FLINT
TOOLS
FIELD GUIDE

FLINT TOOLS
FIELD GUIDE

IDENTIFYING STONE AGE TOOLS

ROBERT TURNER

The
History
Press

First published 2024

The History Press
97 St George's Place, Cheltenham,
Gloucestershire, GL50 3QB
www.thehistorypress.co.uk

British Library Cataloguing in Publication Data.
A catalogue record for this book is available from the British Library.

ISBN 978 1 80399 711 7

Typesetting and origination by The History Press.
Printed and bound in Great Britain by TJ Books Limited, Padstow, Cornwall

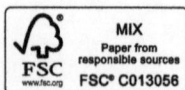

To my wife Gillian, without whom this book would never have gone to print, and to the members of Worthing Archaeological Society who helped.

CONTENTS

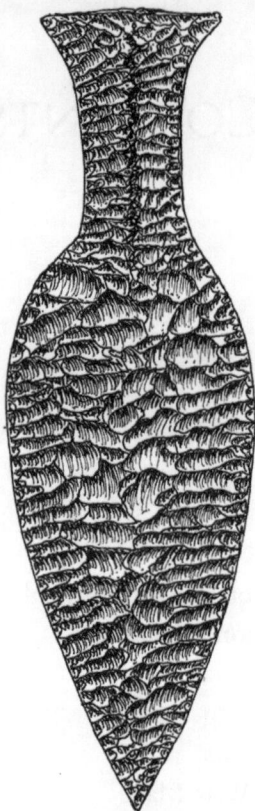

Type 4 Danish dagger.

A FIELD GUIDE TO RECOGNISING FLINT TOOLS

A tool can be described as an object used to assist in the performance of a task. There are many examples of this in nature: an animal using a stick to winkle out a grub from a small crevasse or an otter pounding a shell with a rock to obtain a meal. Tools come in many guises but what delineates a thinking process is the actual manufacture of the tool rather than utilising a found object.

The breaking of a rock deliberately to obtain a sharp edge for the purpose of cutting appears to be the first sign of modifying an environment and goes back many millions of years. These early tools are called eoliths and were first discovered in Kent, in the south of England, by an amateur archaeologist in 1885.

The fact that eoliths were so crude led some to believe that they were actually formed naturally; however, sceptics were gradually convinced that they were man-made as more and more evidence was discovered – in particular, genuine early Lower Pleistocene Oldowan tools found in East Africa.

Oldowan tools were very basic and mainly fashioned by chipping the edges with another stone. They were used by ancient hominins (early humans) across much of Africa during the Lower Palaeolithic period, 2.6 million years ago, until at least 1.7 million years ago. These were followed by the more sophisticated Acheulean industry associated with Homo Erectus, who first appeared about 2 million years ago.

Following Homo Erectus we have a selection of hominin species including Homo Habilis, Homo Heidelbergensis, Neanderthal and, about 60,000 years ago, our species, Homo Sapiens. The final area of the Earth to be populated was the Americas following the Devensian Ice Age from 16,000 to 18,000 years ago.

Each of these groups produced stone tools but they are now identified by different names and different named periods. While the Palaeolithic appears to be a general name for before the last Devensian Ice Age, later periods tend to be named from geographical area to geographical area. For example, the USA uses Paleo-Indian; Early, Middle and Late Archaic; Early; Middle and Late Woodland; and Mississippian, while in Britain we have Early and Late Mesolithic; Early and Late Neolithic; and Bronze Age.

Another point that must be considered is latitude as ice ages have come and gone, with seven in the last million years. With these ice ages came ice sheets that scoured the land and also made huge differences in sea levels up to 140m, all of which revealed or flooded land. Where the ice did not quite reach, the land became a polar desert and thus was devoid of human life and finds during ice ages.

Stone tools can be found in most parts of the world. Some were made, used and then discarded, while others were retained; therefore, simple cutting tools and scrapers are plentiful, while others such as hand axes were retained for continuous use until worn out or broken, and so are found less frequently.

This then is the background to finding stone tools. Like finding fossils, it can be a great delight to pick up and hold something that was made thousands or tens or hundreds of thousands of years ago. Many years ago, I was working on an archaeological site on the Boxgrove horizon where we found four axe-sharpening flakes dated to 495,000 years ago. Holding something that was made and then buried half a million years ago was magic and the feeling has lived with me ever since, so I would like to share this experience.

We all take a great delight in finding things, be it at a car-boot sale or from a walk in the countryside, so this book is a guide to help with finding our past, recognising flint tools and being able to tell in what time period they were made.

INTRODUCTION

Inbuilt in all people is a liking for finding things. Haven't we all picked up the coin we spotted on the pavement, or the seashell on the beach, or the attractive stone we saw in the countryside or field? Treasure hunting is in all of us, especially when we're on beaches such as those in Dorset or Yorkshire where we can hunt for fossils.

We are all guilty of collecting at some stage of our life.

Everyone enjoys going to museums to view items that have been collected over the years that bring to life our ancestors: how they lived, what they wore, what they made and why their possessions were so different to ours. The further we go back into history, the greater the attraction.

In our dim and distant past we are all descended from primitive societies of hunter-gatherers and cave dwellers, and then the early farmers who signalled the beginnings of civilisation. Unless they built in stone, there are few artefacts or finds from these earlier prehistoric periods, so the older the civilisation, the less we know about it.

Natural materials like wood or bone decay and rot, leaving little trace unless conditions are conducive to preservation, and we are left with flint and other stone materials that survive virtually unchanged, so tools made by our ancestors can be found by us today.

Flint, chert, basalt and volcanic glass (obsidian) are just some of the materials called cryptocrystalline because they have no inherent structure and can pass a shock wave. This means they will split along the lines of the shock wave when struck and can be shaped with accuracy to form tools, while other stone materials like granite have to be pecked with small removals to form a shape. Obviously, Stone Age people utilised whatever stone was local and other stone materials had to be imported or traded.

A tool is something that is made to perform a specialised task, so bashing tools look different from cutting tools, as do piercing and scraping tools, with each requiring a different manufacturing process. The tools Stone Age people needed for tasks such as cutting or scraping were very easily fashioned and readily disposable, so they were made, used and then discarded, while other tools like axes were retained or kept, which may account for the numbers of each type we find. To explain this, a single strike produces a sharp blade, while to replace the edge of a dulled blade requires quite a bit of work, so it is easier to make, use, throw away and make a new one.

We can find used and broken tools by looking in places where our ancestors may have lived or for signs of tool production if we discover a manufacturing site. This book is all about how to recognise these finds, how to tell if they were man-made and to give some idea of when they were made.

How To Use This Book

After finding a flint make sure it's clean before examining it carefully, following these steps:

1) Check its characteristics, especially the bulb of percussion and the platform (page 18).
2) Examine it closely for secondary working (retouch).
3) If it either does not have (1) or (2) or has both, it's not a tool or debitage.
4) Try and identify it from the pictures and notes (pages 31–86)
5) Try and establish its time period from the chart (pages 25–28)

Note some tools like side scrapers are found in all periods, so more investigation will be needed, while tools like barbed and tanged arrow heads are only in the Early Bronze Age.

1

BASIC RECOGNITION
OF A STRUCK TOOL

When a flint is struck and fractures, a shock wave is created
and radiates from the point of impact in the form of a sinusoidal wave. As the fracture travels through the knapping
material it loses amplitude, which means the first bit of the
wave is larger than the subsequent waves; this is called the
bulb of percussion.

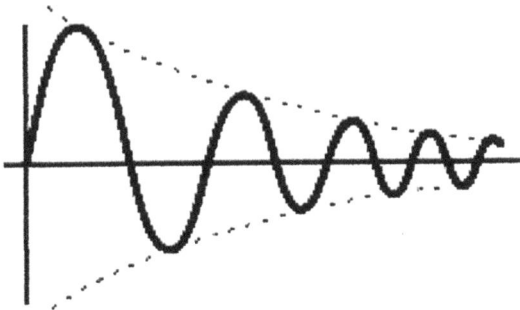

Fig. 1. Reducing sinusoidal wave.

If the knapping material is pure, this fracture will travel in a straight line, but if there are variations or inclusions in the material this can alter the path of the fracture.

To ascertain if your flint has been struck deliberately it must have several elements:

- A platform: the place where it was struck.
- A bulb of percussion: a protruding bulge immediately below the platform
- A series of smaller ripples running parallel and at right angles to the platform and bulb.

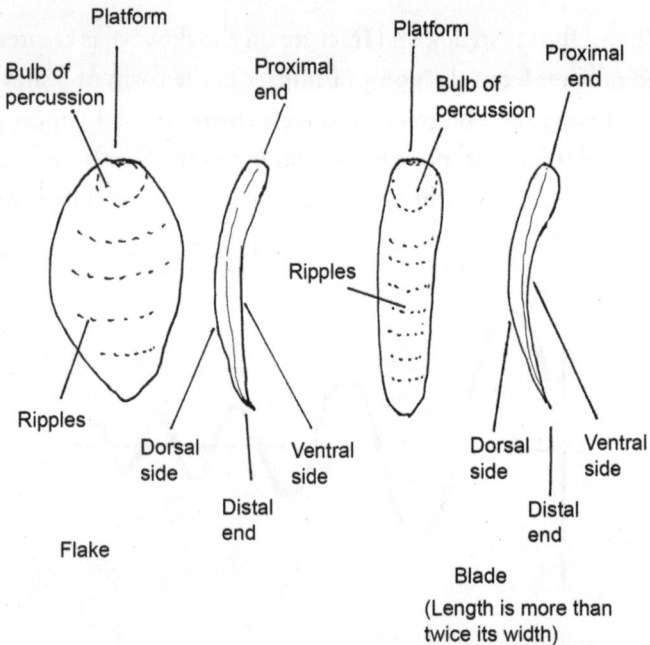

Fig. 2. Flake and blade characteristics.

Sometimes these continuing ripples are very slight but by running your finger down the flint from the bulb you can feel them. Also the bulb may have smaller scars where tiny flakes have sheared off.

If you want to see a perfectly formed scar where a flake has been taken off cryptocrystalline material, have a look in your kitchen at any chipped glass or china plate because each tiny chip is what we call a conchoidal fracture. Look closely at the scar on the glass or plate and you will find it's the reverse of a flake because glass can be knapped.

For those who like technical details, the correct terminology for describing a flake or a blade (a flake with parallel sides where the length is more than twice the width) is shown in Fig. 2.

The tools are in three categories: core, blade and flake. A core tool is where a nodule of flint has been knapped continually, leaving the final tool exposed. Blade and flint tools are from the secondary working of the blades and flakes that have been removed from a core.

When blades or flakes have been removed they will have an extremely sharp edge and this is a tool in its own right and can be used instantly for cutting. To show that they have been used as a tool (we call this utilisation), you have to examine the edge very closely and you will find it has tiny scars that are on both sides of the edge.

You can hit a piece of any flint-type material until you make a flake and use it to cut a piece of wood, examining the edge both before and after use. Flint will get bumped and battered by ploughing and natural wear and tear over the years, but you will find that this scarring is different from a deliberately utilised edge. A cutting edge will have regular scars along the used edge, whereas natural scarring of different sizes is random.

Where a blade or flake is secondary worked it can be from pressure flaking in the manufacturing process. This is done with hand tools where continuous flakes are pushed off a newly struck edge. If the angle of removal is very acute this is referred to as invasive retouch (used for cutting edges) and where the flakes are at a large angle this is called abrupt retouch (used for scrapers).

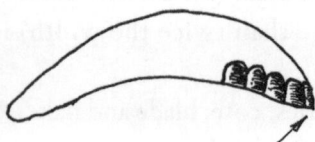

Abrupt retouch to
form a scraper of up
to 70–80 degrees

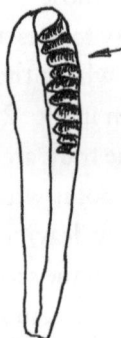

Invasive retouch to
form a cutting edge
of 10 degrees or less

Fig. 3. Retouch: invasive and abrupt.

Sometimes, invasive retouch on tools is really tiny working so you need to inspect the edges carefully or, better still, look with a small magnifying glass. Core tools, on the other hand, like an axe or an adze, will be covered in many scars, as multiple flakes were removed to produce the required shape.

Who Made the Flint Tools?

The origins of our early ancestors is a subject that's still at the front line of research and therefore are being updated continually as new discoveries are made. The early origins of humans go back several million years and current evidence indicates that we originated in Africa with tool production of Homo Habilis, Homo Erectus, Homo Heidelbergensis and then Homo Neanderthalis, a species that in northern Europe became extinct roughly 30,000 to 40,000 years ago. Starting around 60,000 years ago, Homo Sapiens began to spread across the globe, reaching northern Europe as Neanderthals began to decline. The last area to be occupied was the Americas some 13,000 to 18,000 years ago.

For the British Isles and similar latitudes in northern Europe, occupation was deferred until 11,000 to 12,000 years ago. For countries bordering the North Atlantic there were a further several hundred years of ice age because of the Younger Dryas period when the Gulf Stream was diverted by the volume of fresh water from the receding Devensian Ice Age.

The first dwellers to return to the British Isles in the Late Upper Palaeolithic were mainly in the south of England and, due to the returning climate with warming conditions, were mainly living in caves. The Final Upper Palaeolithic saw an increase of population and occupation, spreading northwards by 10,000 years ago in Britain. Then followed the Mesolithic hunter-gatherer period, the Neolithic early farmer period and then the Chalcolithic (Copper Age) and Bronze Age.

The north-eastern part of Europe suffered badly from repeated ice ages in the last million years. This part of the world had only been habitable for about 30 per cent of the time, so for some of the time periods recognised across Europe the northern reaches have been polar deserts.

In the last million years we have undergone some seven ice ages. An example of this can be seen in southern France, where there was an active landscape during the Solutrean period (22,000 to 17,000 BP (Before Present)),while Britain remained a polar desert.

Fig.4. Periods of Habitation in Britain

Time BP (in 000s)	Temperature	Ice Age	Land type	Species (Homo ...)	Time period
750–650	Warm	Cromarian	Peninsular	Erectus	Palaeolithic
650–600	Cold			—	Glacial
600–550	Warm			Heidelburgensis	Palaeolithic
550–500	Cold			—	Glacial
500–470	Warm			Heidelburgensis	Palaeolithic
470–420	Cold	Anglian		—	Glacial
420–360	Warm	Hoxian	Island?	Neanderthal	Palaeolithic
360–340	Cold		Peninsular	—	Glacial
340–280	Warm	Purfleet	Island?	Neanderthal	Palaeolithic
280–240	Cold	Wolstonian	Peninsular	Empty	Glacial
240–180	Warm	Aveley	Island	Neanderthal	Palaeolithic
180–130	Cold	Ipswichian	Peninsular	—	Glacial
130–70	Warm		Island	—	Animals, no humans

Time BP (in 000s)	Temperature	Ice Age	Land type	Species (Homo ...)	Time period
70–50	Cold	Devensian	Island	—	Palaeolithic
50–30	(Cool)			*	Glacial
30–20	Cold		Peninsular	—	Palaeolithic
20–10				Sapiens	Glacial
10–5.4	Warm	Flandrian	Island	Sapiens	Mesolithic
5.4–4.6			formed 8,200	Sapiens	Neolithic
4.6–2.7			years ago	Sapiens	Bronze Age

* Devensian Interstadial? Neanderthal or Sapiens, unsure.

From this chart you can see the periods when people were living in northern Europe.

Because encroaching ice sheets scoured the land during an ice age, only ice-free areas have produced early finds. In Britain, they have been found at Happisburgh (pronounced Haze-boro) 950,000 years ago, Pakefield 700,000 years ago, Boxgrove 495,000 years ago, Clacton 490,000 years ago and Swanscombe 300,000 years ago.

The chances of finding any of these early flint tools are remote but very occasionally they do turn up. Ninety-nine per cent of all tools found are from the period of the Devensian Ice Age, which for northern latitudes was the last 12,000 years.

The further south you travel, the earlier the finds.

For the Americas, infiltration of people from Asia was either following the coastline or by traversing the ice-free passage between 13,000 and 16,000 years ago. DNA investigations show that there were several migrations, with some people travelling all the way to the tip of South America, while others went to North America only.

There is growing evidence that there was a transfer of long-blade flint technology from northern Europe as the technology for producing Clovis- and Fulsome-type flint blades is absent in Asia or Russia.

Tools from Local Geology

When considering tools, we must realise what was required for the way of life then. Hunter-gatherers required tools for killing or collecting food, tools for making clothing and habitation, and tools for hunting. The farmer, on the other hand, needed tools for food growing and production, so the hunter-gatherer had a nomadic existence while the farmer was more sedentary. All these tasks required tools, so unless they were traded or the stone material imported, people had to use what they could find locally.

Your nearest library or museum will have information on the local geology or you may find a regional geology book in your local bookshop or online, so it is relatively easy to find out what types of stone there are locally. Chalk and limestone will sometimes contain flint or chert, and obsidian can be found in volcanic areas.

2

Tool Identification Information

Abbreviation of Time Periods		Years Before Present
EP	Early Palaeolithic	1,000,000 to 150,000
P	Middle Palaeolithic	150,000 to 40,000
LP	Later Palaeolithic	40,000 to 12,000
LUP	Late Upper Palaeolithic	14,000 to 13,000
FUP	Final Upper Palaeolithic	13,000 to 12,000
EM	Early Mesolithic	12,000 to 7,000
LM	Late Mesolithic	7,000 to 6,000
EN	Early Neolithic	6,000 to 5,300
N	Middle Neolithic	5,300 to 4,900
LN	Late Neolithic	4,900 to 4,200
EBA	Early Bronze Age	4,600 to 3,600
BA	Middle Bronze Age	3,600 to 3,200
LBA	Late Bronze Age	3,200 to 2,700

Note. In many books, BC/BCE is used, so there can be a 2,000-year difference between that and BP.

These dates are only a guideline to the changes in prehistory. For example, the transition from hunter-gatherer to farmer took a considerable amount of time and there would have been a period when people were farmers for only a part of the year and hunter-gatherers for the remainder. The flint tool kit therefore changed with these activities as different tools were required for specific tasks. The chart below gives an overall picture of what tools were used and in what periods. Some tools, such as scrapers and knives, are found in all periods with variations in tool technology. Other tools, such as barbed and tanged arrowheads, are specific to one period: the Early Bronze Age.

In earlier periods the population was small, based on the family unit, so there were large differences in the ability to make tools as young children could have been producing them. In later periods the population consisted of larger groups, so it is likely that specialisations existed as daily living tasks became shared. In the Early Bronze Age there was probably a specialist within the community of people who manufactured highly specialised tools.

Fig. 5. Tools by Period (Abbreviated)

Tool/Debitage Types	Paleo	FUP	EM	M	LM	EN	N	LN	EBA	BA	LBA
Adze			▓	▓	▓						
Arrowhead, barbed and tanged									▓		
Arrowhead, chisel								▓			
Arrowhead, leaf-shaped						▓					

Tool/Debitage Types	Paleo	FUP	EM	M	LM	EN	N	LN	EBA	BA	LBA
Arrowhead, laurel						■					
Arrowhead, oblique								■			
Arrowhead, petit tranchet								■			
Awl				■	■	■	■	■	■	■	■
Axe, flaked	■	■	■	■	■	■					
Axe, polished								■	■		
Blade	■	■	■	■	■	■	■	■	■		
Blade, retouched	■	■	■	■	■	■	■	■	■		
Backed tool	■	■	■	■	■						
Biface	■	■				■					
Bladelet	■	■	■	■	■	■					
Borer	■	■	■	■	■	■	■	■			
Bruised blade	■	■									
Burin	■	■	■	■	■	■	■	■			
Chisel					■	■	■	■	■	■	
Chopper	■				■	■	■	■	■	■	■
Cleaver	■										
Combination tool		■	■	■	■	■	■	■	■	■	
Core, single platform	■	■	■	■	■						
Core, bipolar			■	■	■	■	■	■			
Crested blade		■	■	■	■	■	■	■			
Dagger								■	■	■	
Denticulate	■	■	■	■	■	■	■	■			
Fabricator					■	■	■	■	■	■	
Hammer stone	■	■	■	■	■	■	■	■	■	■	■
Knife	■	■	■	■	■	■	■	■	■	■	■
Knife, backed	■	■	■	■	■	■	■	■	■		
Knife, discoidal								■	■		
Levallois tool	■										

Tool/Debitage Types	Paleo	FUP	EM	M	LM	EN	N	LN	EBA	BA	LBA
Mèche de forêt			▓	▓							
Microlith	▓				▓						
Micro burin					▓						
Micro denticulate					▓						
Notched piece	▓	▓	▓	▓	▓						
Ovate	▓	▓									
Pick				▓							
Piercer	▓	▓									
Piercer, Zinken	▓	▓									
Point, Cheddar	▓	▓		▓	▓						
Point, Levallois	▓			▓							
Punch	▓	▓									
Rod						▓	▓	▓			
Scraper, button									▓		
Scraper, discoidal								▓	▓		
Scraper, end	▓	▓									
Scraper, hollow			▓	▓							
Scraper, horned									▓		
Scraper, horseshoe						▓					
Scraper, end, on long blade	▓	▓									
Scraper, side	▓	▓	▓								
Sickle						▓	▓				
Utilised piece										▓	
Y tool						▓	▓				

One of the things to think about before we look at individual tools is that illustrations in books invariably show the perfect tool as pristine as the day it was made. However, the tools you are likely to find were probably discarded as broken or worn. Broken tools may have been thrown out by adults or by children learning to make them. No tool was ever made to be thrown away, although some were produced for a single activity before being discarded.

Tools that you may find can be covered in soil or dirt, so they need to be washed as small retouches along an edge can be covered by mud. Also, do not forget these tools have been in the ground for thousands of years and may have suffered damage from ploughing.

We will look at tool and debitage types in alphabetical order as shown on the Fig. 5 chart, but do not forget that the tools you find can be damaged or broken while those shown here are a complete example. Also, remember flint tools, especially those of the hunter-gatherer, were made specifically for killing and for butchering, so you cannot be squeamish about the way prehistoric people lived.

3

Flint Tools List

This section is the expanded version of the previous page list, which gave approximate dates and periods for use.

Adze

This can also be referred to as a tranchet adze and is a wood-working tool from the Mesolithic and Early Neolithic periods.

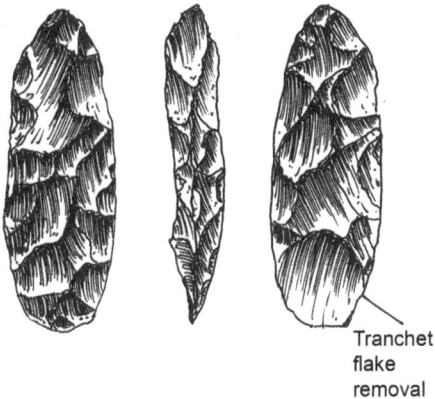

Tranchet
flake
removal   **Fig. 6.**

The adze is mounted on a V-shaped wood handle with the tool cutting edge facing towards you in use. This is a core tool and can vary in size from 10cm up to the largest at about 25cm. It is very difficult to distinguish the Early Neolithic adze from the Mesolithic adze but all have a flat surface at the tool cutting edge. One of the ways to identify an adze is to place the tool on a flat surface as shown.

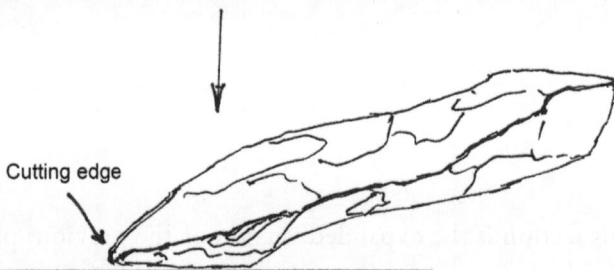

Cutting edge

Fig. 7.

Sometimes adzes can be confused with axe rough-outs, especially in the Early Mesolithic when the cutting face is made from a series of flakes running longitudinally from the cutting edge. These adzes are quite rare as virtually all others have a large single flake taken sideways across the adze, which is why they are termed 'tranchet'.

The removal of a further tranchet flake is a way of resharpening the tool and quite often tranchet flakes themselves can be found. There is a very good video on YouTube by Will Lord showing how an adze is made. He prefers to remove the tranchet flake initially from a flint nodule rather than creating the flake in the final stages of production.

Arrowheads

Everyone wants to find an arrowhead, especially in parts of North America where arrowhead types are prolific.

Bows and arrows in Africa date back to 60,000 years ago but in Europe they do not appear until about 20,000 years ago and, in the UK, not until the return of people after the Devensian Ice Age ended 11,000 years ago. Arrows in the Mesolithic period were tipped with several small flint flakes called microliths, which acted like barbs and will be fully explained later.

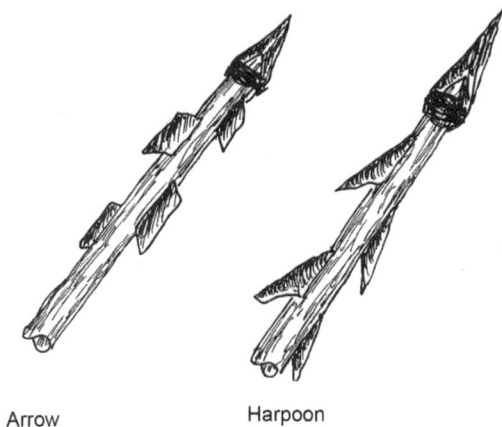

Arrow   Harpoon

Fig. 8.

Single flint arrowheads appeared throughout the Neolithic and the Early Bronze Age and were finally replaced by metal in the Bronze Age. In the North American continent, flint and chert arrowheads were evident from the Clovis era, around 13,000 years ago, into modern times. While Europe only had a few arrowhead types, there are dozens of different styles in America due to the diversity of habitat and individual tribe cultures.

Barbed and Tanged Arrowhead

These arrowheads were predominant in the Early Bronze Age and are relatively difficult to produce but by this time people were living in settlements, so were likely to have a tool-making artisan class of people. Each area tended to have its own specialities but the main types for the southern UK are Suttons, Conygar Hill and Green Low, where the differences are mainly in the lengths of barbs against tangs.

Sutton	Conygar Hill	Green Low

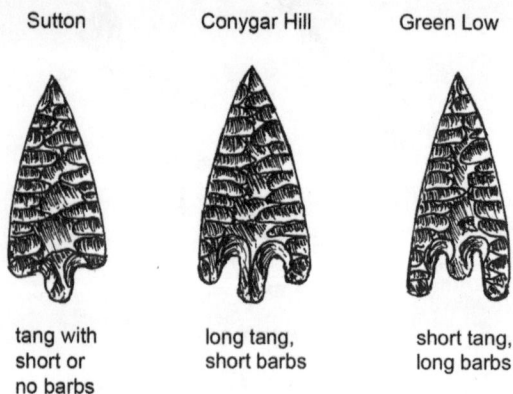

tang with short or no barbs	long tang, short barbs	short tang, long barbs

Fig. 9.

These styles were produced from flakes or Levallois-type blanks. This was the Beaker period, named after the distinct ring-grooved pottery produced at that time.

Some of the arrowheads of this period are beautifully made by overall pressure flaking, while others are less well made from flakes with just retouched edges, possibly denoting the existence of an artisan class of flint knappers.

Many of the barb and tang ends have different shapes, with round, square, angled or pointed ends.

Chisel-Shaped Arrowhead

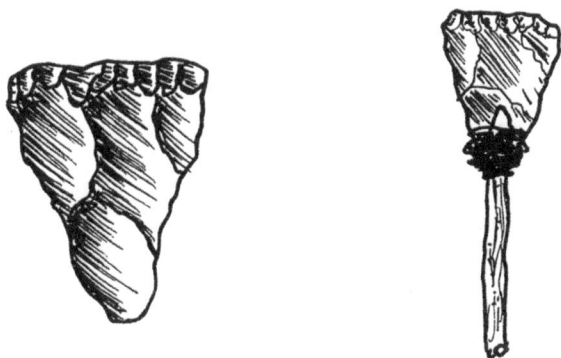

Fig. 10.

Chisel-shaped arrowheads are roughly triangular shaped with a thin base that thickens towards the point. They were mounted on the shaft with the blunt base facing forward and the edges sometimes sharpened or rounded.

When hunting, the expectation is that an arrow with a pointed end makes penetration easier but one with a sharpened flat edge will make a larger entry wound and therefore cause greater blood loss. When an arrow strikes its target, unless it penetrates a major organ, it will not kill the prey immediately but loss of blood can be the deciding factor in a successful hunt.

There is a school of thought regarding the blunted end chisel point that it could have been used for hunting birds where stunning rather than killing would mean the bird was kept alive for a future meal or for egg production by clipping or removing flight feathers to prevent escape.

Leaf-Shaped Arrowhead

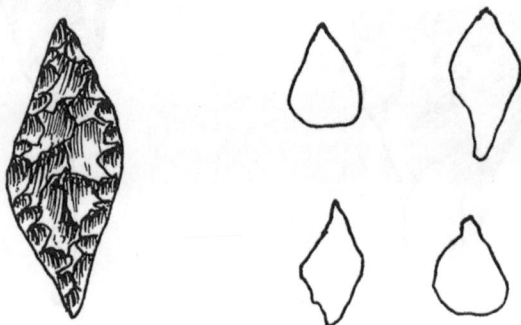

Fig. 11.

With the beginning of the Neolithic period a new type of arrowhead appeared that had better aerodynamic qualities than the previous microlith composite arrow. It was made from an elongated flake in the shape of a tree leaf. All the edges were retouched to make cutting edges. The shapes can be different: some are pointed at both ends and some have rounded bases and are either elongated or squat-shaped.

Quite often, the bulb of percussion has been removed to make mounting on an arrow shaft easier. Some are better made than others and fully flaked, while the plainer types are only retouched around the edges. Do not forget that you may find a used arrowhead so it may have a broken or missing tip. An arrowhead that is broken longitudinally from tip to bulb is an unusual find and may well indicate that it was broken deliberately as some sort of votive offering.

Laurel Leaf Arrowhead

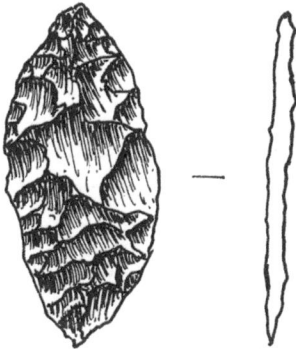

Fig. 12.

This is a bifacially worked tool that looks like a leaf-shaped arrowhead but is made asymmetrically. Its use is still a matter of debate because it is asymmetrical and this rules out it being an arrowhead or a spearhead. It may have been hafted but there is no evidence for this, apart from one side being more invasively worked than the other which could indicate a cutting edge. It is larger than other arrowheads, being between 5 and 9cm from tip to base. Although both faces are flaked, the edges are sometimes retouched while the longer edge is usually invasively retouched.

Oblique Arrowhead

Fig. 13.

This is from the Late Neolithic/Early Bronze Age period. This type of arrowhead was made on a flake, triangular in shape but sometimes not totally symmetrical, and others have a single short barb. They are retouched along one or more edges and some that are more symmetrical have an indented base.

For the first-time finder, it is quite difficult to tell one type of arrowhead from another, but the oblique was mounted point first, so it was different from the chisel point above.

Petit Tranchet Arrowhead

This is very similar to the chisel arrowhead and was used in the same way except that the flake was taken from the side of the rough-out or across the arrowhead.

There are other types or classifications of arrowhead and the level of quality was dependent on the maker. Some arrowheads were made by younger knappers or even children

Fig. 14.

who were learning the skill and so there are inevitably odd shapes that could be used but were not very well made.

Some arrowheads were made with hollow bases to assist with mounting on the shaft and others had asymmetric barbs. One case in point was the Marden arrowhead, which had a greatly elongated single barb, but what the function was is not understood.

Marden point

Fig. 15.

This elongated barb is very fragile and would have broken easily. It was not until 2016, when a complete arrowhead was found, that its true nature was realised. A number of museums had broken barbs in their collections but no one had previously known what they were.

On the European continent there are many variations of arrowheads, with some named after the place of their discovery, but in North America there are a great number of habitat-specific points ranging from the Great Plains and deserts to mountains and coastal regions.

Awl

This tool is similar to a piercer as both are specific types of hole-makers. Where a piercer has a back-and-forth twist motion, the awl can only be twisted in one direction like a modern twist drill.

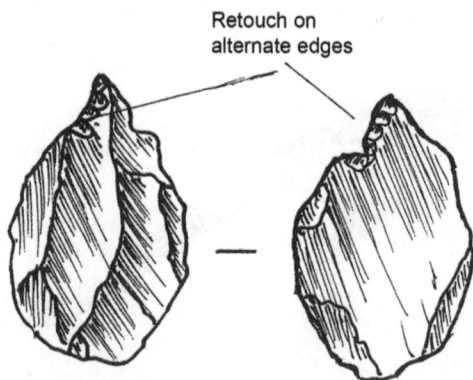

Retouch on alternate edges

Fig. 16.

The awl has a short point with retouch on alternate sides of the point that forms the cutting edge. They are quite rare in the Mesolithic period but more common in the Neolithic and Early Bronze Age.

When they only have retouch on one side of the point, the cutting edge is in the direction of the sharp edge of the retouch scars. You will need to examine both sides around the point for retouch, as they can frequently be confused with piercers that have retouch on each side of the point on the same side of the tool.

Axe, Hand Axe – Flaked and Polished

This is the tool that everyone wants to find – especially a Palaeolithic hand axe of Boxgrove date in Sussex from around 495,000 years ago, through to the post-glacial periods of the Mesolithic and then the Neolithic, when new types of flaked, ground and polished axes were made.

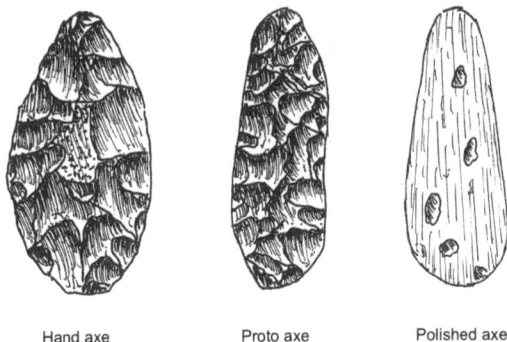

Hand axe   Proto axe   Polished axe

Fig. 17.

Even outside of the well-known archaeological sites, such as Swanscombe, Boxgrove and Pakefield, you can occasionally find hand axes from other eras. (See fig. 4 as to when hominins were in northern Europe.) As the earliest axes or choppers from the Lower Palaeolithic were crudely made and fairly small, they are sometimes difficult to recognise and therefore rarely found, as they only survive in areas where the ice fronts of various ice ages have not reached.

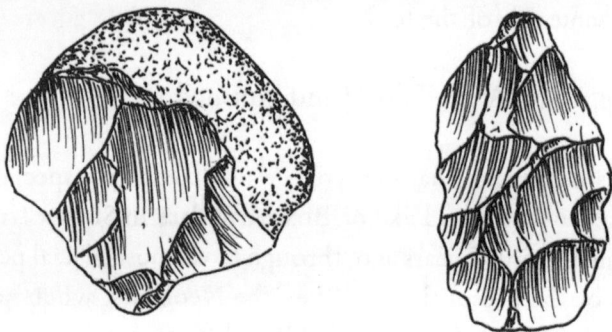

Fig. 18. Lower Palaeolithic chopper and hand axe.

Middle and Upper Palaeolithic axes come in a range of sizes and different shapes. They were produced from flint nodules by systematic flaking to reduce most of the cortex. The chopper was a heavy-duty axe type and was most likely used to dismember carcases rapidly, so it therefore needed to be a robust tool as any kill would attract large predators.

Fig. 19.

Axes from these periods can be pointed, cordate, ovate and heart-shaped or irregularly shaped, like the ficron.

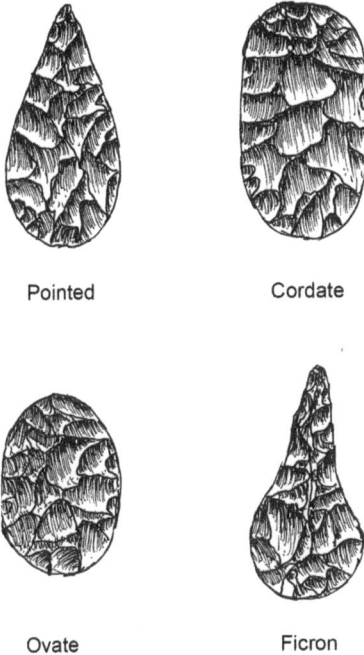

Pointed   Cordate

Ovate   Ficron

Fig. 20.

Axes from the Neolithic period are found more commonly. This type of axe was produced in three stages. A rough-out was produced from a nodule at an axe production site and shaped roughly to remove as much of the unwanted waste material as possible. It was then probably traded, perhaps locally or further afield, when it would be partly finished as a preform. The last stage was the finished flaked axe.

  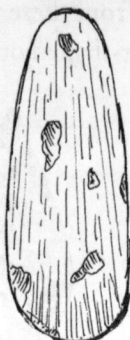

Rough-out   Flaked axe   Polished axe

Fig. 21.

A flaked axe could have been used as a tool at this point or it could be further modified by partial or total polishing. All axes of this period were hafted.

Part-polished   Full-polished

Fig. 22.

Axes were discarded for several reasons: if they were broken while in use, if they could no longer be sharpened, or if there were flaws in the stone during manufacture, or they could simply be lost items. Finding a complete axe is therefore a rare event unless it was from a burial or perhaps an offering.

More commonly found is an axe-sharpening flake. There are two different shapes depending on the type of axe: a radial flake from the tip of the axe or a tranchet type, which is a flake removed from the side edge.

Blade

Blades, both worked and not worked, together with flakes, are the most common tools for all the periods and constitute the most common finds.

The definition of a blade is when the length is more than twice the width and it is struck from a blade core (see Cores). If a blade is less than 12mm wide it is called a bladelet. As demonstrated in Fig. 2, the inner side of a blade is called the ventral side and the outer side is the dorsal side. The base or where it was struck is the platform, next to the bulb of percussion on the ventral side. The platform end is the proximal end of the blade and the far end is the distal end (easy to remember as it is the 'distance' end).

A struck blade in the first instance was not a tool but waste material or 'debitage'. However, a struck blade could be used as a simple cutting tool without further alteration or modification. If the cutting edge has indications of use, such as tiny nicks or notches, then the blade becomes a tool and termed a 'utilised blade'. A magnifying glass is usually needed to determine this. If you view the cutting edge face-on, any tiny notches will be distributed randomly on both sides of the edge and are different from a retouched or reworked blade, where the removals are from one side only.

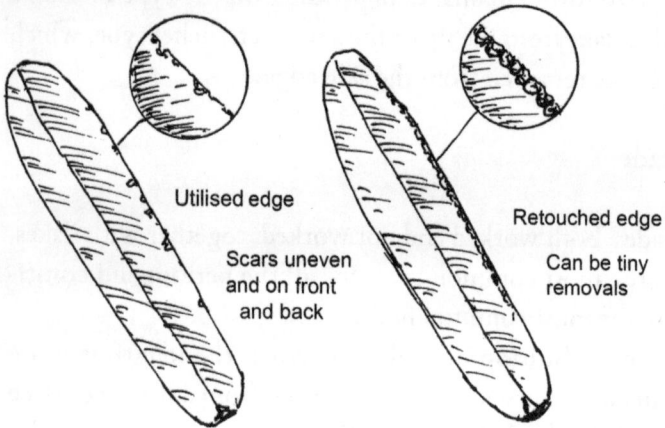

Utilised edge

Scars uneven
and on front
and back

Retouched edge

Can be tiny
removals

Fig. 23.

When a blade or bladelet is reworked or retouched it can take several forms depending on the specific task for which the tool was required.

A blade can have invasive retouch to sharpen the edge, as in a knife.

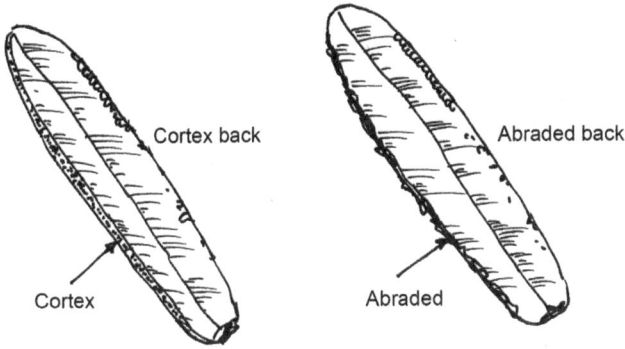

Knife cutting edge retouched or utilised

Fig. 24.

Abrupt retouch is used to make a scraper and is only found on thick blades that have a flat or concave underside (also see Scrapers).

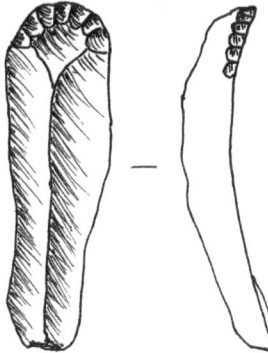

Fig. 25. Abrupt retouch.

A notch is used to cut or scrape a cylindrical object like an arrow shaft.

Notch must be
worked inside

Fig. 26.

A blade can also be pointed to make a piercer (although piercers are more commonly made on flakes).

Point worked
on both sides

Fig. 27.

Blades can be modified to make burins (see Burins section) or reworked and broken to make microliths (see Microliths section).

In the Upper Palaeolithic 'long-blade technology' flourished and this extended into the Mesolithic period, from which you can find scrapers on the end of long and bruised blades.

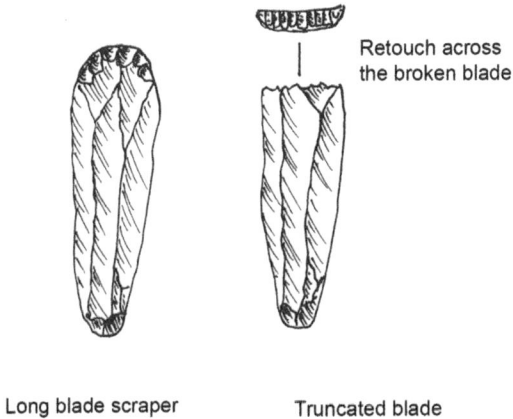

Retouch across
the broken blade

Long blade scraper

Truncated blade

Fig. 28.

When striking blades from a core sometimes they can break into two or three pieces if the shock wave is disrupted.

Backed Tool

When removing a blade from a core it is possible to ensure that where you strike will retain cortex on one side of the blade. This can be very useful as it gives a blunted edge so as not to cut your hand when using the blade as a tool.

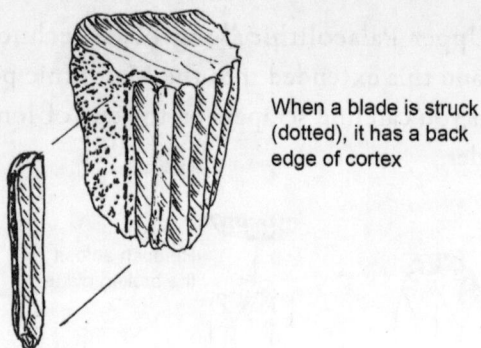

When a blade is struck (dotted), it has a back edge of cortex

Fig. 29.

Alternatively, one edge can be deliberately abraded to produce a blunt edge with the same result.

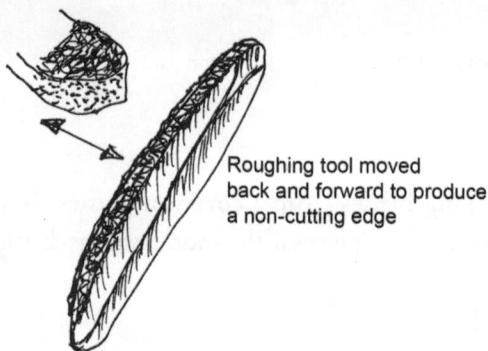

Roughing tool moved back and forward to produce a non-cutting edge

Fig. 30.

Biface

This is the name given to a tool made from a nodule or a large, thick flake. It is oval-shaped or slightly pointed, flaked on both faces and sharpened all around the edge. It is another name for a Palaeolithic hand axe or a Neolithic ovate and could also be found in the Mesolithic, when they may well have been hafted.

Bladelet

Bladelets are small versions of blades, being less than 12mm wide. They appear in the Upper Palaeolithic and Mesolithic periods and were used to manufacture microliths (see Microliths). Discarded broken bladelets with one or two small notches can indicate microlith production.

Waste material
at either end of blade

Fig. 31. With blades (over 12mm) the tip was often modified and used as a microlith.

Borer

This tool is found in most periods up to the Early Bronze Age and is a tool used to increase the size of existing holes in various materials. It resembles a flat-ended piercer.

Each side of the elongated 'nose' is retouched. When retouch is on the same side, this facilitates rotation in both

Fig. 32.

directions. When the retouch is on alternate sides then it acts like a modern drill and can only cut in one direction.

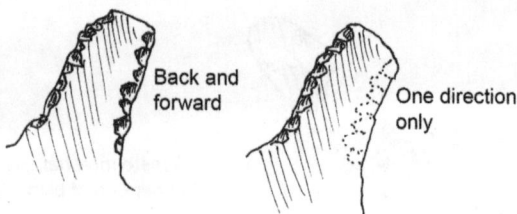

Back and forward

One direction only

Fig. 33. Retouch same and opposite sides.

Higher quality of flint and care taken in manufacture usually denote an earlier period. Borers are not found as frequently as piercers but must have been part of the same tool kit (see Piercers).

Bruised Blade

These are only found in the last stages of the Upper Palaeolithic and are the last of the Solutrean 'long-blade technology'.

They are large, heavy, scarred and abraded blades that may have been used as chopping tools.

Fig. 34. Bruised blade.

Burin

These are often referred to as 'gravers' and are found in the Upper Palaeolithic up to the Early Neolithic. Their use is not fully understood but they may well have been used to make grooves or slots in bone or wood as part of composite tool manufacture.

The burin has two cutting edges at an angle of 90 degrees or just above this angle with two removals. The second removal can produce a tiny spall that looks like a small bladelet. There are many different types of burin, including the bulb end of a blade that has been discarded in the making of blade tools.

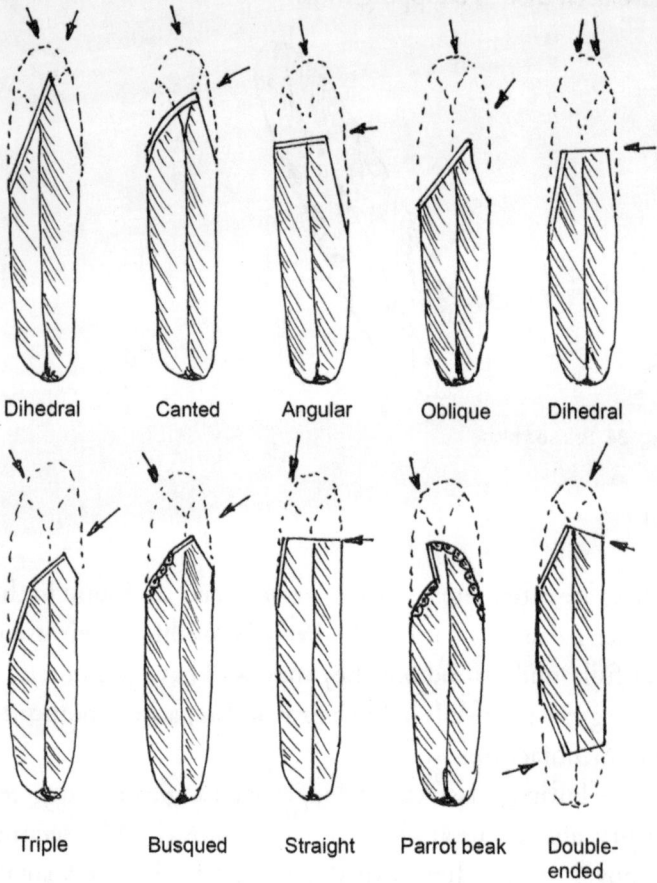

| Dihedral | Canted | Angular | Oblique | Dihedral |

| Triple | Busqued | Straight | Parrot beak | Double-ended |

Fig. 35. Different variations of burins.

Chisel

This tool is found in the Early Neolithic to the Early Bronze Age. It is like a very thin axe with parallel sides, fully flaked and even polished. The cutting edge is bifacially flaked and the opposing end is squared off.

The production of chisels is very similar to Neolithic axe manufacture. They are quite rare finds and, as with axes, some are in the rough-out stage and others are flaked and polished.

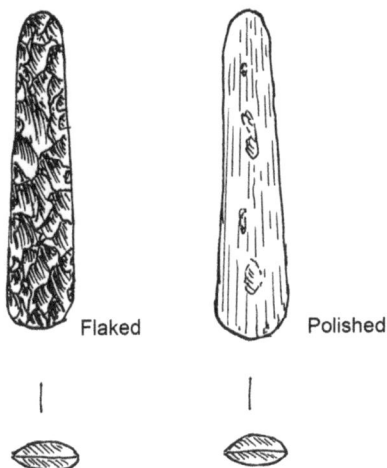

Flaked   Polished

Fig. 36.

Chopper

Chopping tools have been used in all periods but it is difficult to identify their specific periods because generally they are crudely made. In some periods they are just pebbles or nodules with two or three flake removals to produce thick cutting edges. They were heavy-duty tools and may well have been used to dismember a carcass quickly or some other activity.

In the Late Neolithic period, ovates with cortex remaining on one side may have been used as choppers, and towards the end of the Bronze Age, any likely discarded tools or large flakes from earlier periods were reused .

Earlier Stone Age

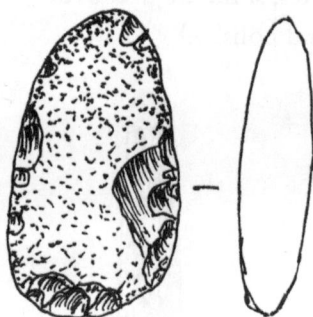

Fig. 37.

Late Neolithic

Cleaver

In the earlier part of the Palaeolithic, cleavers were similar to choppers but better made and flaked on both sides. They have the appearance of ovates, with one end narrower than the other, and are often mistaken for hand axes. Again, they were heavy-duty, robust tools.

Fig. 38. Cleaver.

Combination Tool

In most periods there are tools that have two and occasionally three different task-specific types on the same blade or flake, and these are known as combination tools. They are multi-purpose tools, probably equivalent to our modern Swiss Army knives.

Combinations of scrapers, piercers, awls, notches and burins are most common. Double-ended fabricators can also be found, as well as combined knives and denticulates.

Notch scraper   Piercer scraper   Knife notch

Fig. 39.

Core, Single Platform

There are two different types of cores: flake cores and blade cores. Generally, blade cores are earlier and were produced in the Upper Palaeolithic, Mesolithic and Early Neolithic periods.

A blade core is usually made from a good-quality flint nodule that has been quartered to produce a flat surface. This surface then becomes the platform for all removals. Initially, the cortex is removed and then a series of blades can be struck around the perimeter of the platform, which tends to produce a cone-shaped core.

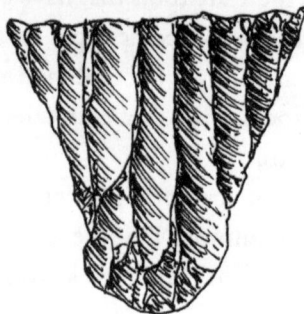

Fig. 40. Single platform core.

The ridges on the core are from the previous blade removals and quite often you find that the previous removal terminated halfway down the scar in a hinge fracture. This is because there was insufficient striking force, which resulted in the shock wave failing halfway through the removal. When these terminations occurred, the core was probably discarded because hinge fractures are difficult to remove.

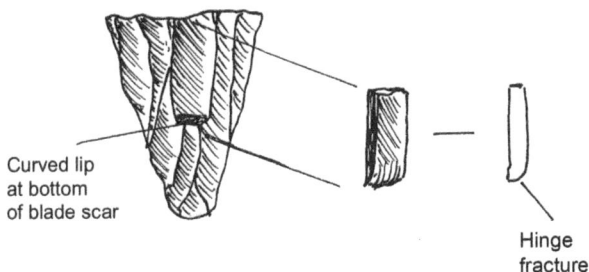

Curved lip
at bottom
of blade scar

Hinge
fracture

Fig. 41.

Core, Bipolar

When a core is struck for blade or flake production from two or more different places around the core it is described as bipolar, or when the core was struck in one direction and then turned 180 degrees to remove blades from opposing end.

During the Neolithic period, the best flint for producing cores was obtained by mining but by the Late Bronze Age any suitable piece of flint was used.

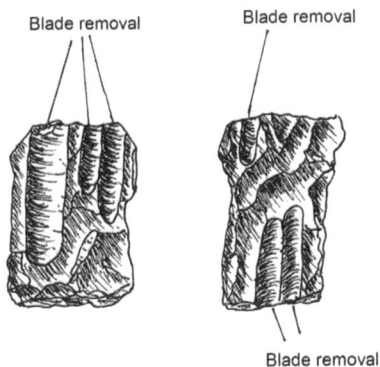

Blade removal

Blade removal

Blade removal

Fig. 42.

Cores are not regarded as tools and are classified as debitage or waste material because they do not have a tool function.

Crested Blade

This is a carefully prepared thick blade with a central ridge or crest and is triangular in cross section. When a core was being prepared for blade removals, this blade would be the initial blade removed to leave ridges on the core for further removals. Crested blades are sometimes used as fabricators (see Fabricators).

Fig. 43.

Dagger

Daggers are rare in the UK and mainly found in northern parts of Europe, especially Denmark. They appear in the Late Neolithic and Early Bronze Age, at a time when the metals copper and then bronze were first introduced. These metals were rare and costly in prehistoric terms, so it is probable that high-quality flint replicas were an alternative.

Daggers come in many variations of length and width. The early types found in the UK tend to have either points at both ends or a point and a flat end.

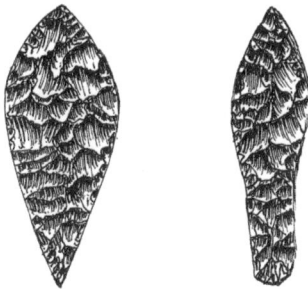

Fig. 44.

In northern Europe, flint daggers became more intricate to the point of replicating even the stitching on the leather handle of a metal dagger. The skill and care of dagger manufacture indicates a specialist class of flint knapper.

The full range of daggers is classified from types I to IV with sub-variations.

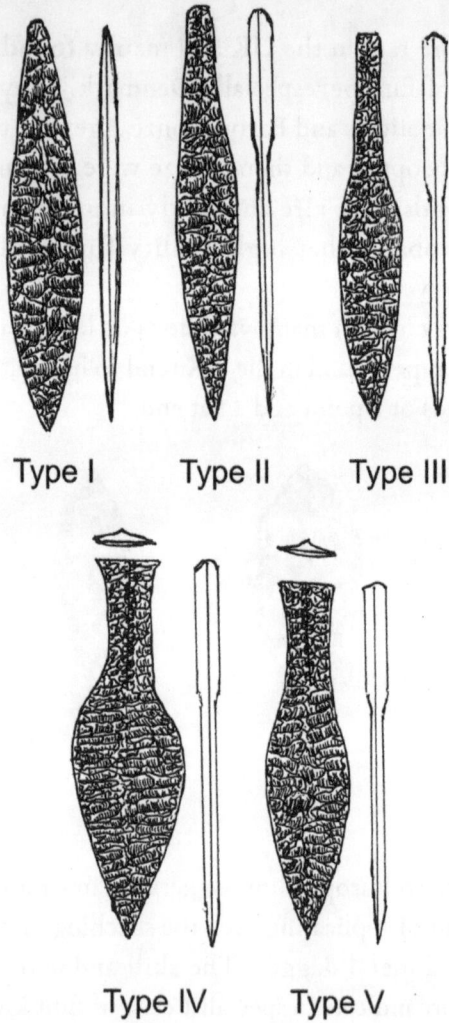

Fig. 45.

Denticulate

This is a blade or a flake that has been turned into a serrated or saw-type tool. A straight edge on the flint is retouched at 90 degrees to make a series of evenly spaced jagged peaks. Close examination of the scars on the underside edge will show that they are circular rather than elongated retouch scars used to sharpen the blade or flake.

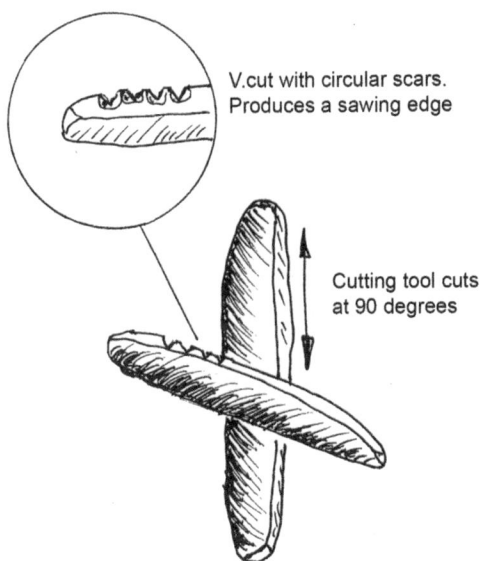

V.cut with circular scars. Produces a sawing edge

Cutting tool cuts at 90 degrees

Fig. 46.

They are made by taking two flints with sharp edges and cutting one edge into the other at 90 degrees. As the peaks are cut evenly, the denticulate will cut like a saw with a forwards and backwards cutting movement.

Fabricator

Many books describe fabricators as 'strike-a-lights', thinking they were used for fire lighting, but modern experiments show that these are retouched tools made for a specific task. They are hand tools and used to produce retouch by pressure flaking.

They are made on thick blades or flakes with one flat side and the other heavily crested or ridged and triangular in cross section, or fully flaked with a square, oval or roughly round cross section.

Fig. 47.

The ends can be pointed, beaked or rounded and often show signs of considerable wear.

Hammer Stone

The main tool for striking off flakes or blades is a hammer stone. This can be a rounded nodule of flint or other hard stone and is recognisable by multiple scars produced by the act of hammering. Hammer stones can sometimes be broken, so it is not unusual to find discarded pieces with multiple scars.

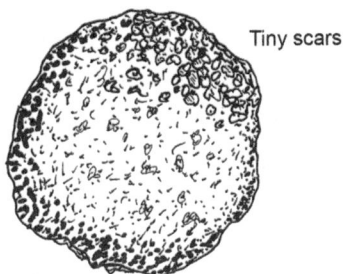

Tiny scars

Fig. 48.

Hammer stones were used for tool production in all prehistoric periods and some discarded stones are known to have been reused in the Late Neolithic period to burnish pottery.

Knife

There is a certain amount of confusion between knives, blades and cutting tools because all can be used for the

Fig. 49.

same purpose. Knives are usually made on blades and can be simple, unmodified blades or retouched. When an unmodified blade has been used it is termed 'utilised' and can be identified by small nicks on both sides of the blade, whereas retouch is only on one side of the blade.

Shouldered knives are where one blade edge has an opposite partially abraded or cortex edge to make handling easier. (See Blade and Backed Blade.)

From the Early Neolithic to the Bronze Age, knives were flaked on a thicker blade and shouldered with one edge sharpened and the back edge blunted. These knives are rare in the UK and can be confused with shouldered points.

Knife, Discoidal

In the Late Neolithic to Early Bronze Age, circular bifacial flakes were ground and polished (or partially polished) to make discoidal knives. Sometimes, they were not always completely sharpened around the edge.

Fig. 50.

Levallois Tool

Found in Levallois-Perret, Paris, in the nineteenth century, Levallois-type tools first appear in the Middle Palaeolithic, 250,000 to 300,000 years ago, as a Neanderthal tool, but reappear again in the Late Neolithic/Early Bronze Age for making arrowhead blanks. Strangely, this method of making arrowheads also appears much later in North America, especially in Missouri and the White River areas.

There are two types of Levallois tool. First, a nodule was radially flaked, then one end was removed to make a platform from which a completed chopping or cutting tool was struck.

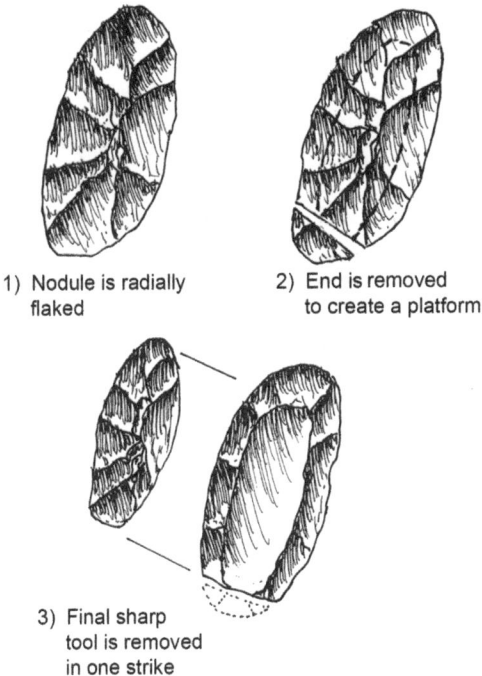

1) Nodule is radially flaked

2) End is removed to create a platform

3) Final sharp tool is removed in one strike

Fig. 51.

In the Late Neolithic/Early Bronze Age, the same technique was used but the resulting tool was shallower and smaller.

The second technique was used only in the Palaeolithic period and involved removal of two flakes at different angles from the top of a nodule to create a long crest. One end of the crest was then removed to make a platform and the first flake was struck and discarded. The second and subsequent flakes would result in ready-made points or arrowheads.

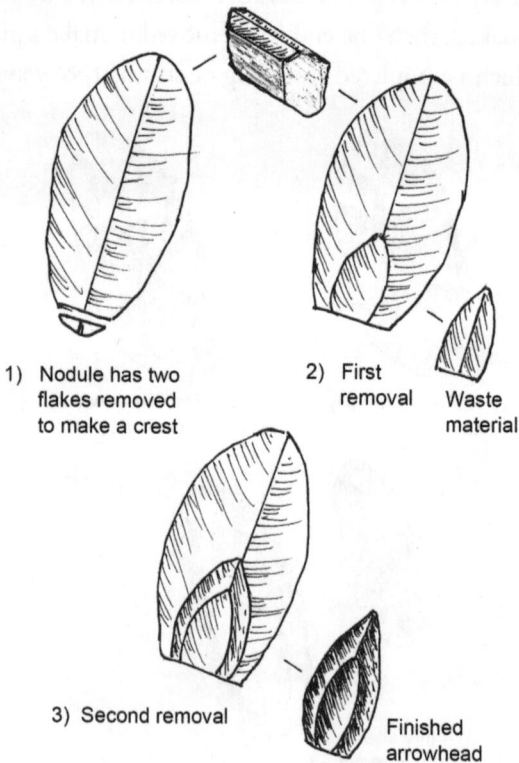

1) Nodule has two flakes removed to make a crest

2) First removal   Waste material

3) Second removal   Finished arrowhead

Fig. 52.

Mèche de Forêt

In the Mesolithic period there was a distinctive type of very fine piercer on a small, thin bladelet. This was abruptly retouched along both edges to form points at both ends and was used for drilling very small holes.

Some *mèches de forêt*, translated as 'matches of the forest', can be slightly wider with one rounded end.

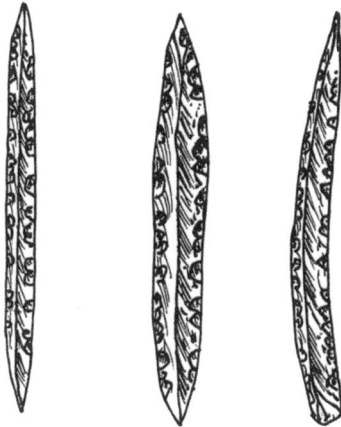

Fig. 53. See the coloured plates for size compared to a £1 coin.

Microlith

After the long-blade technology of the Upper Palaeolithic, composite tools were made using small retouched flakes and blades to produce points and barbs.

These tools appear throughout the Mesolithic period and come in all sorts of shapes and sizes. They were inserted into shafts to make arrows and spears or other composite tools like harpoons.

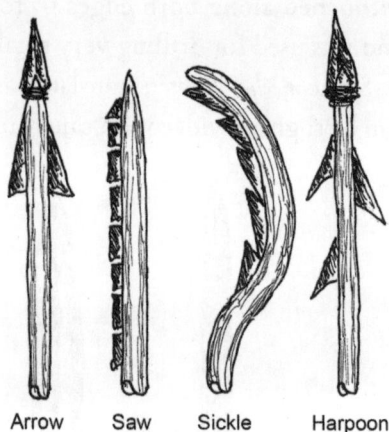

Arrow   Saw   Sickle   Harpoon

Fig. 54.

Microliths are usually reworked but sometimes it can be difficult to tell as they can be worn through use. Each microlith was glued into a slot in a wooden shaft to form a barbed tool and, when it was no longer sharp from wear, it was replaced, so it is often the case that you may have discovered a discarded worn microlith. Quite often, archaeological knapping sites are found where not only microliths were being manufactured for new tools but also maintenance of existing tools was being carried out. So, discarded and worn microliths can be found as well as debitage from the production process.

Over the years there have been several classifications to try to describe the various shapes of microliths. Some descriptions are obvious, including boat shape, pear shape and crescent, but most descriptions refer to geometric shapes such as trapezoidal, isosceles and rhomboid, as well as convex, scalene, symmetrical and asymmetrical.

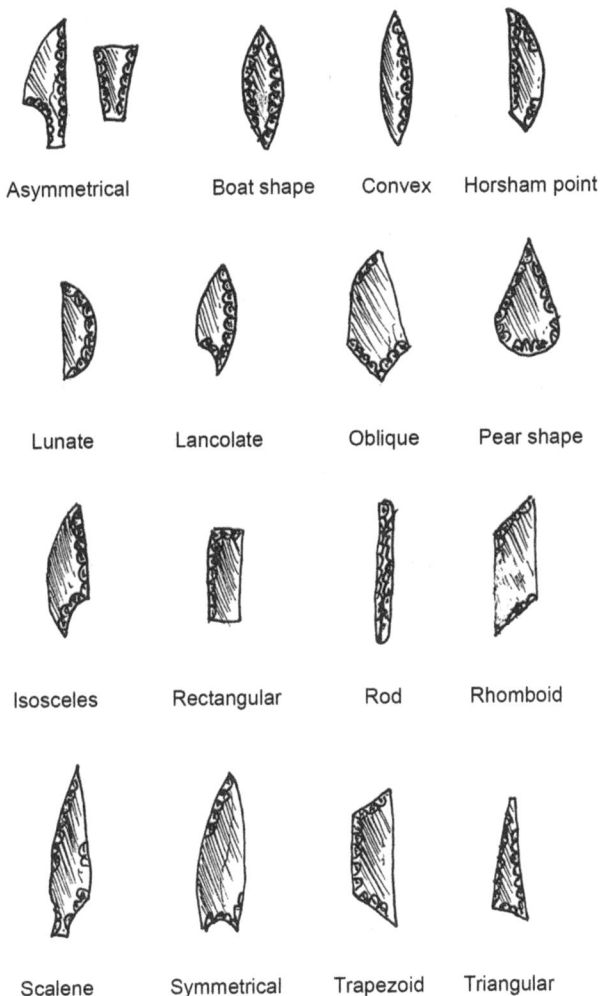

Asymmetrical	Boat shape	Convex	Horsham point
Lunate	Lancolate	Oblique	Pear shape
Isosceles	Rectangular	Rod	Rhomboid
Scalene	Symmetrical	Trapezoid	Triangular

Fig. 55.

Because of the diversity of microliths, it is difficult to use shapes as a dating method.

Micro Burin

It is uncertain if this was a tool or a waste product from microlith manufacture. It is the proximal end of a used bladelet with what appears to be a small hook. If it was a tool, it is a strange one and its use is not understood.

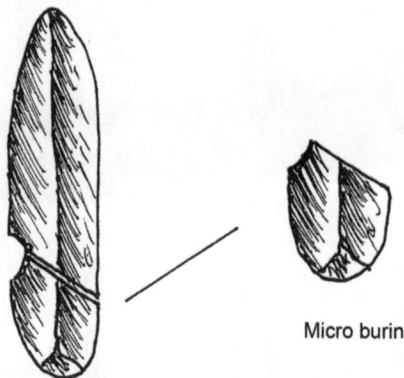

Micro burin

Making the microlith

Fig. 56.

Micro Denticulate

This was made on a small blade with either a straight or curved edge with tiny notches and was used as a saw tool. The notches were made at 90 degrees by using a second blade and therefore the scars are circular (see Denticulate).

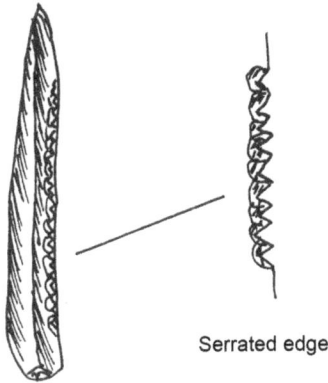

Serrated edge

Fig. 57.

These tools appear to be too small for use but it is possible that several could have been mounted in a slot of wood or bone to make a longer saw.

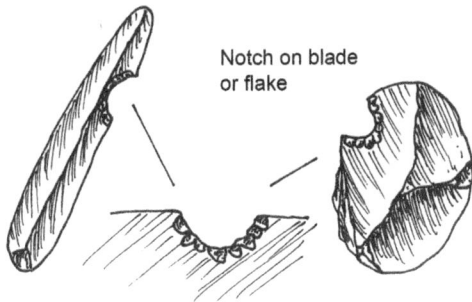

Notch on blade or flake

Fig. 58.

Notched Piece

This tool can be on a blade, flake or formed as a combination tool with another type, such as a scraper or piercer. The notch is internally retouched and was probably used to remove bark for arrow shafts or larger hafted tools. Although notches can occur from plough damage, these blades or flakes are not regarded as tools unless the notches are retouched.

Ovate

The ovate appears first as a hand axe in the Palaeolithic period. It is a fully flaked, slightly flattened circular flint and is a rare find. It is slightly smaller than the cordate hand axe, which tends to be more pear-shaped, and there is no indication that it was hafted. This type of tool appears again in the Upper Palaeolithic, around 45,000 years ago, and then finally in the Late Neolithic/Early Bronze Age. However, this later ovate does have some retained cortex.

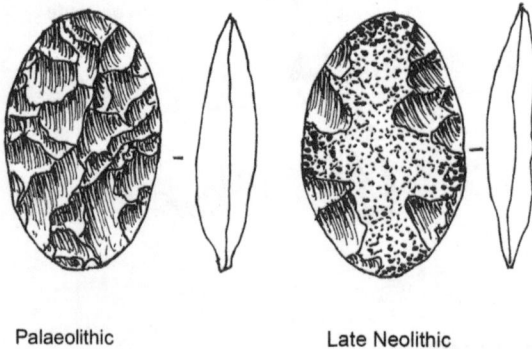

Palaeolithic   Late Neolithic

Fig. 59.

Pick

Picks are crudely made tools with usually large amounts of retained cortex. They can sometimes resemble axe rough-outs but the main difference is that one end of a pick is pointed. Picks were used as 'grubbing out' tools in the Mesolithic period and may have been handheld or hafted. Sometimes they can be quite small, from 8 to 10cm long.

Fig. 60.

Piercer

This tool is found in all periods. It was the hole-maker of the Stone Age and, together with the scraper, it is found in large numbers as it was easily made on both natural and retouched points and often discarded. It can also be one of the tool types formed as combination tools.

Piercers were used by a twisting backward and forward movement and were therefore retouched on only one side of the point, either on one or both edges, and are not to be confused with awls, which were retouched on alternate sides.

They were made on small flakes or the ends of blades that were knapped to produce a point and then retouched. Bronze Age piercers have extended necked points that are easily identifiable.

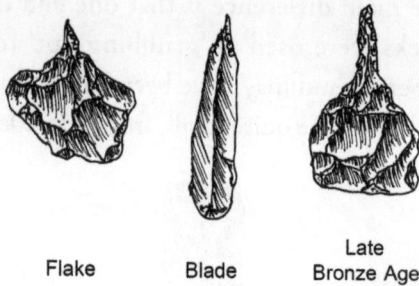

| Flake | Blade | Late Bronze Age |

Fig. 61.

Piercer, Zinken

The term coming from the German for 'prongs', this is a distinctive piercer from the Later Palaeolithic. It was produced on a thick blade with the reduced neck offset at an angle.

Fig. 62.

Point

In the Americas points can cover a whole range of tools, including arrowheads and spear points, while in the UK they mainly relate to tool types of the Palaeolithic and Mesolithic, so it is really a matter of terminology in different cultures.

The first use of bows and arrows in Africa was probably some 70,000 years ago, while in more northerly climes, 20,000 to 25,000 years ago is the current best guess for the appearance of arrowheads. However, the earliest spear point may have been the Neanderthal Levallois point (see Levallois Tool), followed by the start of long-blade technology around 40,000 to 50,000 years ago.

These points were produced on fairly thin blades so that they could be mounted on the end of shafts. For a point to penetrate prey, it requires both edges to be sharpened. Some points may also have a removal or 'flute' towards the base or butt-end, making attachment to the shaft much easier.

The three main types are the leaf-shaped long blade, the shouldered and the Font Robert tanged points. (For other points, see Arrowhead)

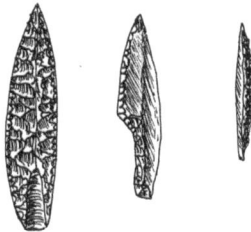

Long blade   Shouldered   Font Robert

Fig. 63.

The Creswellian and Cheddar points are long, trapezoid-alshaped blades with one backed edge but it is unclear how these tools were used.

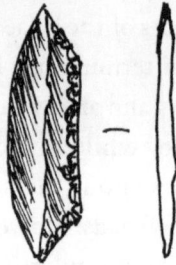

Fig. 64.

Punch and Rod

Up to now we have only considered direct knapping strikes, where the hammer struck the worked piece directly, but occasionally we find straight pieces of bone or flint that were used as punches or rods to remove blades or flakes by indirect percussion. The bone was usually antler with an oval or round cross section and the flint would be a thick, straight, crested blade.

Indirect percussion was achieved by holding the work piece between the knees in a sitting position or between the feet on the ground. The punch or rod was then placed on the work piece and the hammer used to strike off the blade or flake through the punch or rod. In the Mesolithic and Neolithic periods, these tools were often used to remove blades from blade cores.

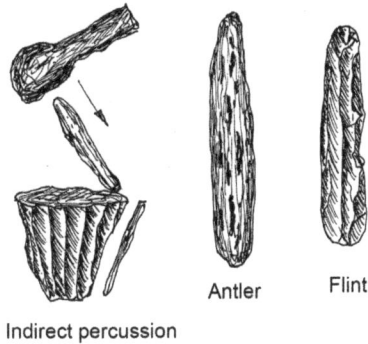

Antler   Flint

Indirect percussion

Fig. 65.

Scraper

This is the most common tool found on Stone Age sites because it was simple to make on any convex or straight blades or flakes. It can be identified by abrupt retouch at an angle of 70 to 80 degrees at the distal end that forms the 'scraping' edge.

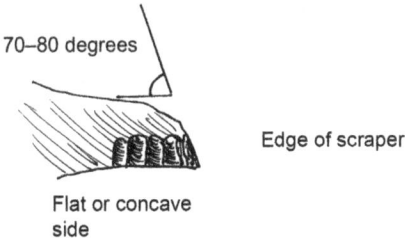

70–80 degrees

Edge of scraper

Flat or concave side

Fig. 66.

This type of retouch enabled fat or hair to be removed from animal hides without causing damage to the hide and was useful for other similar tasks.

Scrapers come in all shapes and sizes and some were probably made for specific tasks. Through use scrapers lose their working edges, so identification of types is sometimes difficult.

Button Scraper
These are small, roughly circular scrapers, also known as 'thumb' scrapers, and date from the Late Neolithic to the Early Bronze Age. They were usually retouched more than 180 degrees around the circumference, so must have been used for very small tasks.

Fig. 67.

Discoidal Scraper
These also date to the Late Neolithic and Early Bronze Age and have the same characteristics as the button scraper above but are larger and sometimes retain some cortex. Retouch can extend around three-quarters of the circumference.

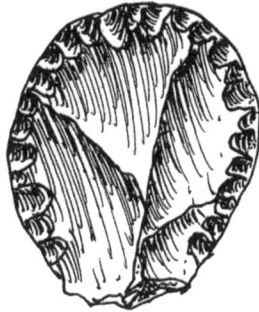

Fig. 68.

End Scraper

End scrapers are found from all periods from the Palaeolithic to the Late Bronze Age, where they can be massive and quite crudely worked up to 8 to 10cm in diameter. The Palaeolithic end scrapers tend to be on sturdy flakes until the Late Palaeolithic, when new technology produced end scrapers on blades, and this continued into the Mesolithic until the Neolithic, when scrapers were produced on various-sized flakes.

Blade   Flake

Fig. 69.

Hollow Scraper

Hollow scrapers usually appear at the end of the Mesolithic up to the Early Bronze Age. They are on flakes that have large concave edges and may have been used for removing bark or other such material from wood. They are quite rare finds.

Fig. 70.

Horned Scraper

The Late Bronze Age has an unusual tool in the form of the horned scraper. It is a large flake with a retouched concave hollow and two prominent points. This was probably used as a scraper but, as the points are about 3 to 4cm apart, it is suggested that this tool may also have been used to score parallel lines on leather to produce strips for binding.

Fig. 71.

Long-Blade End Scraper

Long-Blade End Scraper

In the Late Palaeolithic many scrapers were produced on the
end of a long blade and this technology continued into the
Mesolithic with elongated flake scrapers.

Fig. 72.

Side Scraper

Side scrapers on blades and flakes are evident in all periods
but, from the Neolithic, end scrapers were generally formed
on flakes rather than blades and these became more robust
in the Bronze Age.

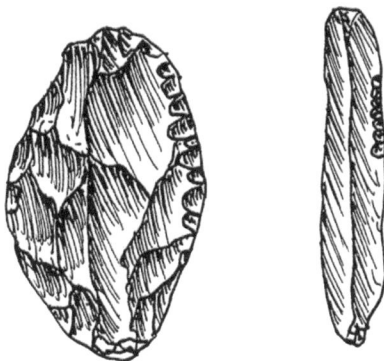

Fig. 73.

Sickle

This tool is significant as an indication of the introduction of farming in the Neolithic period. Early Neolithic sickles were composite tools consisting of small blade sections with abrupt retouch along one edge for hafting into a curved wooden handle. In the Later Neolithic/Early Bronze Age, one-piece sickles were produced on large curved flakes with abrupt and invasive retouch and similarly hafted in curved wooden handles. Both types are rare finds.

Fig. 74.

Utilised tool

From the Neolithic and Bronze Age, we sometimes find pieces of flint with cutting edges that show signs of casual use before being discarded, This wear is indicated by small scars along a sharp or cutting edge.

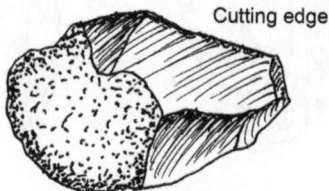

Cutting edge

Fig. 75.

Y Tool

This is an enigmatic tool found occasionally in the Neolithic period. It was made on short, chunky flakes, narrowing at one end to a point and a distinctive 'Y' hollow shape at the other. The hollow and point were usually worked but its specific use is unclear, although it is suggested that it was for stripping bark.

Fig. 76.

★★★

These are the main tool types you are likely to find but there are others you may never come across. They are variations of tools already mentioned but are specific to different continents, an example being the varied arrowheads found in North America.

If you are lucky enough to find something but you are unsure of what it is, there is always someone to help and give advice. In the UK there are many local archaeological societies or your local Finds Liaison Officer of the Portable Antiquities Scheme who would be happy to help and their contact details can be found online.

It is a magic feeling to hold something in your hand that was made thousands or more years ago and once you begin looking and searching you will be amazed at what you can find.

A Mesolithic core.

Type 4 Danish dagger, Bronze Age.

Replica flint blade, Solutrean/Mesolithic.

Mesolithic pick (broken).

Early Neolithic leaf-shaped arrowheads.

Early Neolithic fabricator.

Mesolithic microlith.

Mesolithic piercer.

Mesolithic burin.

Mesolithic combination tool notch/awl.

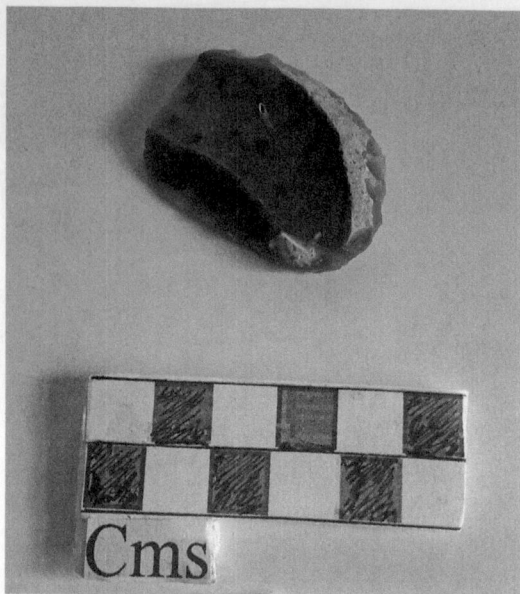

Late Mesolithic/Early Neolithic side scraper.

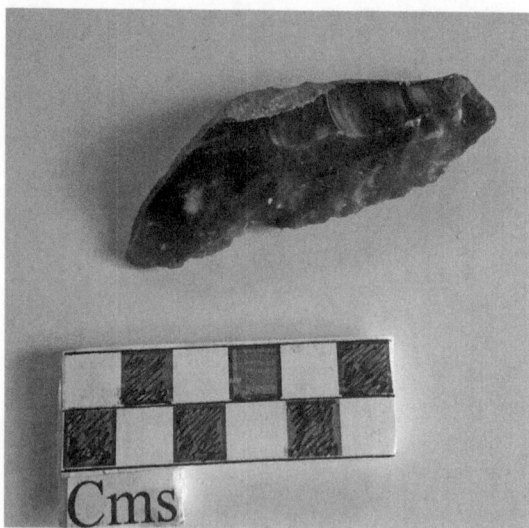

Late Mesolithic/Early Neolithic backed knife.

Early Neolithic backed knife.

Early Neolithic notched flake.

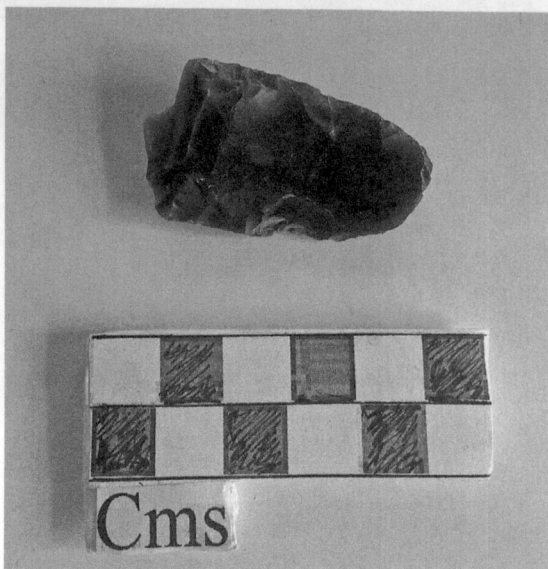

Early Neolithic combination end/side scraper.

Neolithic arrowheads. Left to right: oblique, triangular, chisel.

Early Bronze Age arrowhead.

Late Neolithic/Early Bronze Age piercer.

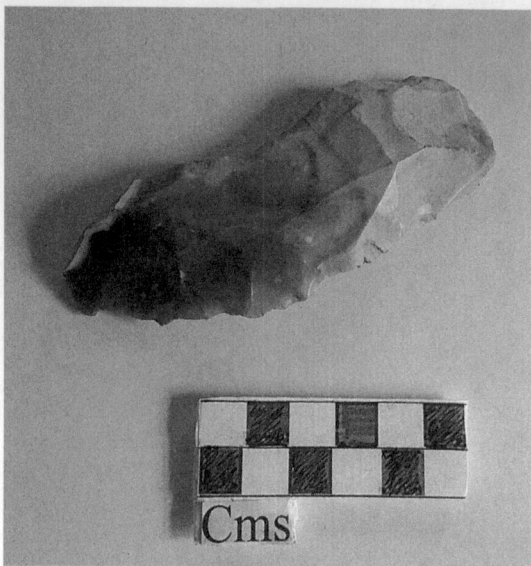

Late Neolithic/Early Bronze Age sickle.

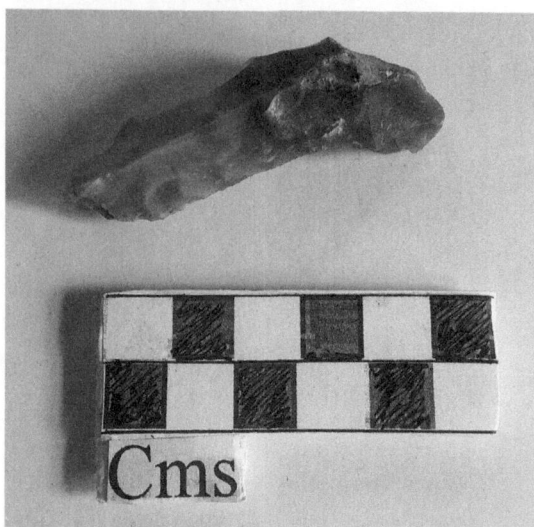

Late Neolithic/Early Bronze Age fabricator.

Two *Mèches de forêt* (matches of the forest), Mesolithic drill bits, with coin for scale.

Neolithic fabricator.

Replica Lower Palaeolithic hand axe.

Lower Palaeolithic hand axe.

Mesolithic adze.

Neolithic end scraper.

Neolithic flaked axe.

Neolithic polish stone/hammer stone.

Late Neolithic arrowheads. Left to right: triangular, hollow base, petit tranchet.

Late Bronze Age chopper.

Late Bronze Age scraper.

Late Neolithic/Early Bronze Age plano convex knife.

Late Neolithic/Early Bronze Age thumbnail scrapers.

Late Neolithic/Early Bronze Age side/hollow scraper.

Flint tools on the ground.

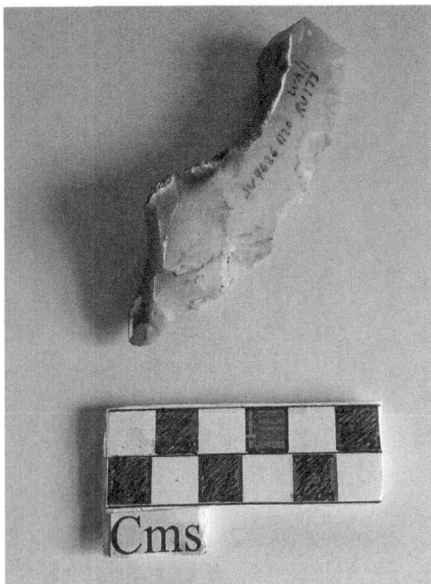

Late Bronze Age piercer.

Late Bronze Age chopper.

Late Neolithic/Early Bronze Age button scraper.

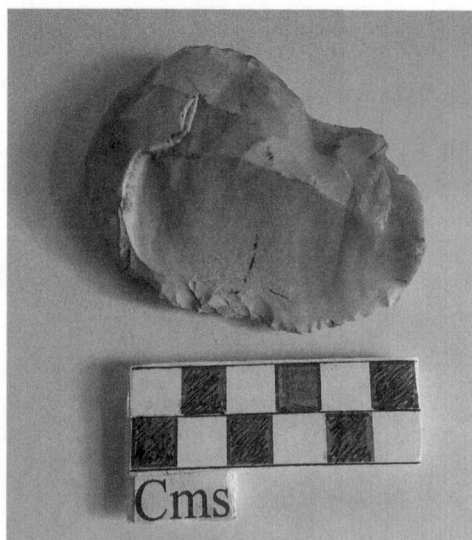

Late Neolithic/Early Bronze Age discoidal knife.

4

WHERE TO LOOK

Where to look for flint tools will depend on where you live, but wherever you are, you can be sure people were there a long time before you. Ploughed fields are a good choice but please ensure you have the landowner's permission to be there. Trackways may well have been in use for hundreds or even thousands of years and can also be good places to look. So, apart from archaeological sites, the answer is virtually anywhere.

Whereas anyone can recognise a coin, as far as flint tools are concerned, you have an advantage insofar as you now know what you are looking for.

Occasionally, you can come across a small area with many struck flakes that could indicate a knapping site. When a knapper was making tools, especially core tools, they had to remove a lot of waste material in the process, which produced quite a number of flakes. It is unlikely that you would find the tools as these would have been taken away when completed, but the discarded waste material would remain.

An example of this is the Boxgrove site, dated to around 495,000 years ago, at the Eartham Quarry, West Sussex, where a knapper knelt on what is now a buried land surface to make flint bifaces and in the process produced waste material that fell in and around their knees. The site became buried by silts and gravels for nearly half a million years but, when it was excavated in the late 1980s, the outline of the knapper's knees was still evident.

Prehistoric knapping sites discovered on archaeological sites are always excavated carefully, as not only is waste material evident, but sometimes discarded broken tools or knapping failures from the manufacturing process can also be found.

Occasionally, an insignificant find from a knapping site can tell a story, much like the small 5cm worked flint nodule found on a Late Mesolithic/Early Neolithic site near the West Sussex coast. The relatively small site was near a newly cut river channel where evidence of blade production was found. Much of the flint used for the process had been obtained from local beach deposits and all the nodules were of very good-quality black flint. However, the small nodule found was tiny and had deliberate but random flake removals. It was therefore thought this may have been the work of a child trying to copy an adult in knapping flint, as the nodule was far too small for an adult to use. This perhaps gives a 'snapshot' of life 6,000 years ago of a family group searching for flint and then sitting and working together to make the tools that would be necessary for their existence.

5

FURTHER VIEWPOINTS

*For further viewpoints I asked some of the members of my archaeo-
logical society to comment about how they started to become interested
in flint and their views on finding and identifying flint tools.*

Martin Simons writes:

Flint Tools My Way

My first introduction to prehistoric flint tools had me
slightly bewildered, I thought, 'I'm never going to get the
hang of this!' But, gradually, with the help of our society flint team, things became clearer, even an obsession,
although there will always be plenty of conundrums in the
recognition of flint tools.

All my experience is based around my local area. We
have, in our archaeological society field unit, been fortunate
to have a local ploughman's lifetime collection of flint to

catalogue and record, as well as flint found on several local society excavations.

Whenever I go for a country walk my family know I will spend much of my time scanning the ground looking for the telltale signs of struck or worked flint. I am still amazed to find prehistoric tools lying on the surface of a footpath or field edge. It would be very unusual not to find something of interest, however, the temptation to pick up and keep everything soon results in a lot of flint with no real purpose other than general interest. To have any useful meaning, it is essential to record the location of any finds and Ordnance Survey Locate is a very useful free app to record map references.

Ideally, find a field that you know has prehistoric interest and seek permission from the land owner to collect from that field, recording everything. Hopefully, a pattern will emerge, a report may be written and conclusions can be drawn. A flint catalogue can be made with tool description, period, cortex, colour, weight, size, quality of flint, quality of working, patination, map reference and any other relevant comments.

What to look for on a field walk? Primarily: shape, colour, texture, anything that looks out of place, including foreign stone, and be alert for the tiny microliths, flakes and burin spalls. On a bright day it is possible to detect a bulb of percussion, ripples, ridges, sharp edges, clean flakes with no cortex, blades and so on.

With experience, a keen eye can soon be achieved. 'Leave no stone unturned' is a relevant saying here. With the current apparent demise of ploughing in favour of cultivators to preserve soil structure, the opportunities for field walking may become fewer in the future.

To aid the study of flint tools, they should be washed carefully and cleaned prior to being examined. Before looking at the finer detail, feel the artefact in your hand and look at it from all angles. Does it hold comfortably? Is it hard hammer or soft hammer, is there any edge preparation, was there a reason it was discarded? Then, with the aid of an eyeglass or magnifier – 10× magnification is ideal – the intricacies of retouch and utilisation can be studied. I find it useful to have a light source to one side to help to show the facets of retouch and other details.

On a typical flint assemblage around 60 per cent may be debitage and 40 per cent tools; tools being our main interest here. Of the tools, about 40 to 50 per cent can only be described as retouched or modified flakes that do not fit any of the recognised tool types satisfactorily. These flakes may have been modified for a one-off purpose, used and soon discarded. My own rule on retouch is for a flake, blade or piece to qualify as retouched there must be at least three consecutive adjoining retouches.

Knives are interesting. A backed knife (back edge abraded, retouched or left as cortex to aid handling) can have a utilised cutting edge (wear from use) or a retouched cutting edge. Similarly, a knife can have a utilised cutting edge or a retouched edge and can be many shapes. Logically, a retouched cutting edge can be compared with a modern steak knife for cutting flesh, but it would not be much use for cutting hide, which would cut more easily with an unretouched cutting edge. This brings me on to alternative and/or logical thinking on the uses of some flint tools. A flake with an end hinge fracture with retouched lateral edges would lend itself to a tool for working fats or brain material into a hide to soften, waterproof or burnish. A horned scraper could be used to score a hide to aid the cutting of a strap with parallel edges; it may not be a scraper at all! A scraper may feel awkward when held in the right hand but held in the left hand it feels usable, hence a left-handed scraper. A tool may have a thumb grip flake taken off the dorsal side to aid handling.

A wealth of information and YouTube videos on flint tools, reports, experimental archaeology, flint knapping, etc., are available on the web. A flint-knapping course will give further insights into the making of flint tools and will certainly give an indication of how highly skilled our ancestors were.

There are many publications with drawings of flint tools and generally these are fine examples. The reality 'on the ground' is that most flint tools are far from being perfect and rarely easy to identify! Identification is often entirely subjective, which is where group discussions are particularly valuable – all part of the challenge of studying flint tools.

Martin Simons

People come to show an interest in lithics from many different backgrounds but always there is that inquisitive trait to find out more about the past and the people who lived it.

Theresa Griffiths writes:

My Journey Towards Learning to Identify Flint Tools

My first experience of lithics was with the television programme *Time Team*, where I enjoyed watching archaeologists, flint experts and flint knappers who stunned the viewer with the ability to find and manufacture flint tools that were the same as the ones found on the digs.

It was also the first time I had come across the phrase 'Experimental Archaeology', so I began to form the ambition to become part of a dig by learning all that I could about archaeology. After retiring from teaching, I started on a two-year course at my local University Centre for Continuing Education. The course provided part-time non-degree students, including school leavers and mature students, with the chance to study archaeology through assignments and dissertations, lectures and study tours. This was my first practical fieldwork and excavation experience and it gave me my first hands-on encounter with flint.

The course fully supported community volunteering, so when I finished the two years at college I joined my local archaeological society and became an enthusiastic amateur voluntary archaeologist. This is where my lithic learning became earnest. I met the finds team and gained experience in small finds and met a flint specialist, the author of this book, a flint expert and a master flint knapper. I began working as part of the finds team and, because flint is a large part of archaeology on many local excavations, I gravitated to the flint group.

I am also living on the Downs overlooking the wonderful Cissbury Ring, the largest hill fort in Sussex and an area of prolific Neolithic flint mines (approximately 290 pits). My house is on an ancient track that leads to the local area of Neolithic flint mining and is opposite a field that may once have been a Neolithic settlement site, although this has been disputed. So, naturally, as my knowledge grew, so did my ability to spot Neolithic tools and flake debitage lying on the surface during my daily dog walks across the Downs.

My first experience of understanding the nature of a worked flint came from learning the difference between flake debitage, a flake that is the result of core reduction, and a tool, a flake that has been modified through knapping to make a knife, a scraper or a piercer. All my first flint finds turned out to be frost fracture or pot lids but occasionally they were actual tools or cores and, when this happened, I was told that I had 'a good eye', which spurred me on to try really hard in understanding and identifying flint tools from different prehistoric periods other than Neolithic.

During our flint work in finds sessions, studying, categorising and cataloguing, I soon came to realise that the flint tools we were finding on our digs and field walks were not like the magnificent examples you see in museums or illustrated in lithic books and journals. The majority of flint found on our sites were not as easy to identify as the ones in the books. Unfortunately, they weren't so beautifully manufactured, some had knapping mistakes and fractures, whilst others had very worn or broken and spoiled edges through water damage or had been broken through ploughing, all of which made them more difficult to interpret.

I really began to admire their quirky, rough appearance and when we find a perfect example of a Mesolithic blade, or partially polished Neolithic axe, the flint group erupts into appreciative exclamations. I have also taken part in several flint knapping practical sessions and certainly appreciate the skill involved, although I recognise that it's not my forte. I find the initial task of detaching a flake from large piece of flint using a hammer stone very challenging. I can select from an assemblage of debitage and shape a simple tool using pressure flaking once the core has been reduced to usable flakes by our expert flint knapper.

I have recently progressed to being part of a team writing flint reports. It has been great fun collaborating with flint-minded folks and a steep learning curve, with our group's expert guides supervising and overseeing our work at every stage. My strong point, and the part that I enjoy the most in writing reports, has been the flint descriptions and drawing. It has taken me a while to learn not to embellish my descriptions and to keep to the observable facts. But it is through examining flints closely, looking at each detail, sometimes under a microscope, for accurate drawing, is where I have come to appreciate the work of the Mesolithic, Neolithic or Bronze Age knapper the most. I have had many 'eureka' moments being part of the flint group and the others in the finds meetings and on some of our digs and field walks. For example, some of my first actual flint tools finds were verified, also finding tiny microliths on a field walk (hands and knees style) in a soggy, deeply furrowed field locally and coming across a group of Mesolithic blades on the bank of a stream in a site not far from the sea. There is always something new to learn. My aim is to have a better understanding of what happened on a site and determine the way of life of the people who passed through or stayed to work the land through studying the distribution of the flint tools and debitage.

Theresa Griffiths

In trying to get as many different views of the interest in flint tools the main attitude that comes across is that we are finding things that someone in the dim and distant past has left us as a part of their lives and that each piece can tell a story.

Jacqueline Lake writes:

When we moved from Scotland to the south of England many years ago, I was unaware of the prehistory visible in the landscape around me and it was entirely by chance that the house we moved into was only half an hour's walk from Cissbury Ring, the second-largest hill fort in England. Around the top of the hill there are areas of bumps and hollows, the remains of more than 200 flint mines, excavated in the Neolithic, long before the ring was built. Scattered around the remains and on the pathways and patches of bare ground where animals have burrowed are lots of flint stones and lumps of chalk.

The geology is very different from what I'd been familiar with in Scotland but I have always been interested in prehistory and evidently a knowledge of flint is necessary to understand how people lived then.

To find out more, I joined the local archaeological society and was pleased to find a very lively group, with a lot going on. Luckily, there are flint experts among the members who have for some years been helping and encouraging others to learn about the use of flint in prehistory.

The first event I attended was an introduction to flint knapping. It was fascinating to watch how easily a skilled knapper produced different tools from flint. I've had several goes at it since and on the few occasions when I have hit the right spot at the right angle to produce a useful piece, it felt good. How exciting it must have been for early humans to discover this skill, which must have played a major part in helping them to thrive and survive.

With practice, I've learned that by holding a worked flint, examining its shape and size, and feeling around it for a good holding position, it is possible to make a good guess at its purpose. Then, by looking closely at each of the scars left by the knapper's removals, you can begin to work out the sequence of the blows made by the knapper and his/her purpose in making them.

Once you start mastering that skill every worked flint becomes a puzzle waiting to be solved. That all sounds so simple, but it is not that easy, particularly assessing in which prehistoric period the tool was made. Luckily, some tool types are produced only during specific periods. Others, however, continue across several prehistoric periods and major lifestyle changes. With practice, you learn to use clues such as the flint quality and the neatness of the knapping, but mainly you gain knowledge by working in small groups and looking at a lot of flints.

Flint recognition is not an exact science and so differences of opinion do occur but half of the joy in doing it is the exchange of opinions, the arguing of your case and eventually coming to agreement.

Early in my learning about flint journey, I was lucky to be given an assemblage of Mesolithic worked flints to examine and identify. I knew very little at that stage and I'm pretty sure I would make a much better job of it now, but the good thing was I was able to handle a lot of flints. The flints were mostly used for hunting and included microliths, bladelets and cores. I found the microliths and the process of their manufacture intriguing. Microliths are small, sharp, finely worked pieces made to be hafted on to a wooden shaft for hunting. They are mostly produced from a bladelet, by breaking off a length and retouching it to obtain the precise shape required. Usually, small nicks are made on the sides to aid the snapping. On digs we do occasionally find bladelets with nicks in them, presumably lost or discarded before use.

The cores from which the bladelets are made are quite distinctive, and easy to recognise as being Mesolithic. They are generally made from good-quality flint and are knapped carefully to maximise the number of bladelets that can be made. We often find small ones that have been depleted so much there is not enough flint left to produce a usable bladelet.

Recently, our society carried out a series of digs at a site located at the foot of the Sussex Downs, a couple of miles from the coast, where we excavated around 2,000 flints ranging from Late Mesolithic to Late Bronze Age. A small group of us created a catalogue of all details of each flint, including assigning each to one of three periods, Late Mesolithic/Early Neolithic, Late Neolithic/Early Bronze age and Late Bronze Age. By analysing the data and taking account of the relevant changes in coastline and climate over the period, we put together a description of the type of activities we considered likely to have been carried out by people coming and going, around the site, over the 6,000 years.

It is very pleasing to use the flint knowledge to gain some insight into local prehistory, but the best thing is the fun of learning alongside likeminded people.

Jacqueline Lake

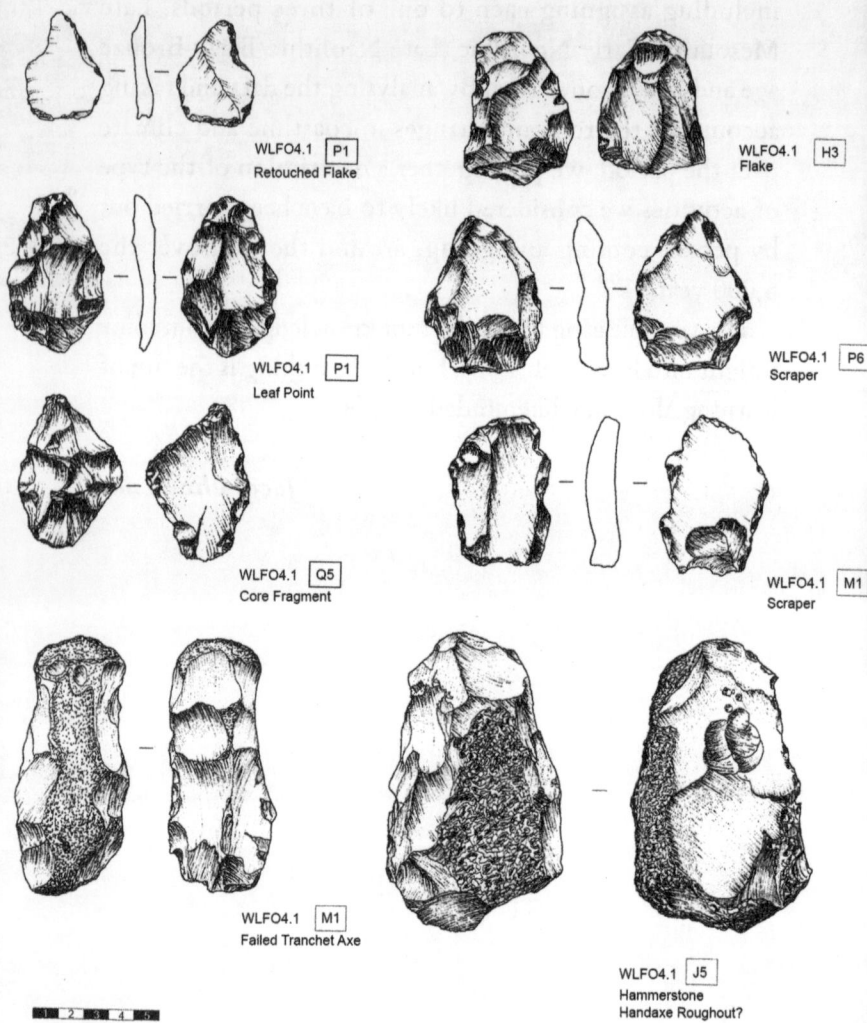

WLFO4.1 [P1]
Retouched Flake

WLFO4.1 [H3]
Flake

WLFO4.1 [P1]
Leaf Point

WLFO4.1 [P6]
Scraper

WLFO4.1 [Q5]
Core Fragment

WLFO4.1 [M1]
Scraper

WLFO4.1 [M1]
Failed Tranchet Axe

WLFO4.1 [J5]
Hammerstone
Handaxe Roughout?

Scale in Centimetres

Fig. 77. Some of the flint tools from on site.

6

How the Tools Were Made

The next logical step if you are interested in flint tools is to have a go at making them yourself, which, if you persevere, is not that difficult, but it does take practice. The best thing about 'having a go' is it can cost you very little to start. Online you can find all sorts of rocks and tool kits for sale but some can be expensive. If, however, you follow these notes, you will be able to at least get started and gain an insight into the basics that you can then build on if you want to take knapping forward.

Here is a list of all the things you need to get started:

A pair of safety glasses or your own glasses.
Several hammer stones of different sizes, as round as possible.
An old piece of carpet for a knee pad.
A chair to sit on and a suitable piece of flint to work on.

There are lots more items that you could have but the above list will give you a basic idea of what is required. Let us take these items one by one.

Flint is very sharp, so eye protection is always a good idea and, if you do not have any eye covering of your own, plastic safety glasses can be purchased in any DIY store.

Hammer stones should be as round as possible and can be picked up on many beaches. You will need a range of sizes from cricket or tennis ball size down to a large marble. Garden centres usually stock pebbles and, if you ask nicely, you can probably buy three or four pebbles for less than £1.

Knee pads can be from any old piece of flexible carpet measuring 20 by 50cm (stiff carpet as used in car mats does not work) or use a double thickness if necessary.

Flint is cryptocrystalline, which means it has no structure and will therefore carry a shock wave, which is how the rock fractures. If you do not live in a flint area, many other materials will knap like flint, such as obsidian, glass, bottle bases, ceramic tiles and even old ceramic kitchen sinks.

A Word of Warning

It is always preferable to work in the open air because of flint dust.

When you start knapping, flint or other material will leave many tiny sharp flakes, so putting a sheet down (especially if you are on grass) before you start is a good idea. It is also very important to clear up after a knapping session, especially if there are children or pets around. Also, find a safe place to put your waste material: either bury it or take it to your local recycling centre.

How It Works

The shock wave generated by a strike running through the work material as a sinusoidal wave that diminishes in amplitude as it travels. If you want to see what a conchoidal fracture and a percussion wave scar look like take a look in your kitchen cupboard at any chipped glass or plate with a magnifier to see the detail.

How to Start

To begin knapping, if you are right-handed sit on an upright chair, place your carpet pad on your left knee and hold the piece to be struck in your left hand on the pad (the reverse for left-handed people).

How and where to strike? This is the where many people fail and get disillusioned, so we need some tuition.

1) The problem of striking with some force is that to begin with you will have difficulty with muscle control, so you usually miss the spot you were aiming for. While you can tap with accuracy, the use of force usually elongates your length of swing, so you will usually hit further into the flint than the target point. You just have to practise!
2) If you are trying to remove a flake, the target place where you strike must be less than 90 degrees.

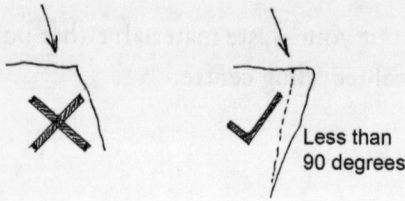

Fig. 78.

3) This striking angle is crucial as the shock wave radiates in a percussion cone at 50 degrees to the line of the strike, so you have to adjust the position of the flint on your knee to get the right angle.

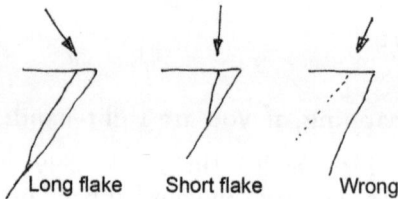

Fig. 79.

4) If the force of the strike is insufficient, the shock wave will not be strong enough and will fade and finally escape outwards as a hinge fracture.

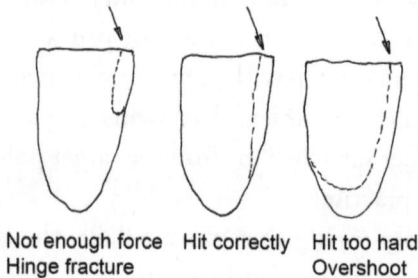

Fig. 80.

I know this all sounds rather complicated but if you try to get it right you will be surprised how quickly you can master the technique. If you strike your flint and nothing happens, then review these four points and try again.

If you get it right, you will hear a sharp crack and your first flake will drop off. Have a close look at your first success and note the platform where you made your strike, the bulb of percussion where the first sinusoidal wave started and the resulting ripples. Be careful as the edges of your flake are very sharp.

Congratulations! Now do it again. You will soon understand how using different size hammer stones works.

When you have removed several flakes, choose two that have sharp edges and turn back to Fig. 46: Denticulate, and make your first tool by using one edge as a cutting tool to make notches with the other flake as shown. It is as easy as that!

If your piece is rounded and covered with cortex you have to break into the nodule to get started, which will require some force. Cortex does not carry a shock wave and can vary in thickness. Once you have broken through, you will find hitting the exposed flint produces much better results.

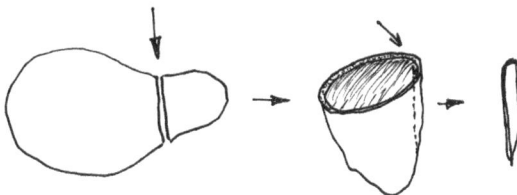

Fig. 81.

You will have to keep knapping until you have produced a reasonable number of flakes but remember that each flake is potentially also a tool in itself that can be worked further to produce a piercer, awl or burin.

To carry out secondary working or retouch, you need to add two tools to your tool kit: a hand pad and a pressure flaker. The best material for a hand pad is thick leather or several layers of leather as long as it is strong enough to make sure you cannot pierce your hand if your pressure flaker slips. You will be surprised at where you can get odd pieces of leather (roughly 10cm by 10cm). For example, from an old discarded boot or shoe, an unused hand bag or an offcut from any leather object. Alternatively, an old mud flap or any thick, flexible material is good. Take a look at internet videos of knappers working and see what they use.

Your pressure flaker has to be made of bone, antler or copper (do not try to use brass or steel). If using copper, this needs to be a rod of pen or pencil thickness and at most 10 to 15cm long or shorter if inserted into a handle. I have used a 6in copper nail in a file handle for years (for some strange reason, nails are still sold in imperial measurement). Alternatively, you might be able to buy copper at your local scrapyard at scrap value and then find an appropriate handle at your local DIY store. The working end of the flaker must be filed to a point like a pencil and slightly rounded at the end.

Again, for right-handed people place the pad in your left palm with the work piece on top.

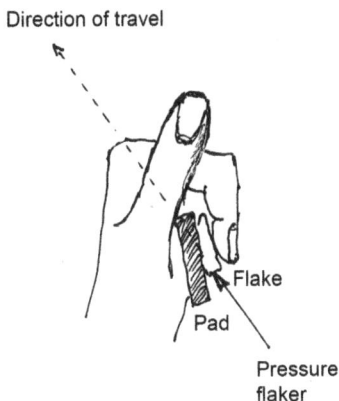

Fig. 82.

To produce the pressure flake, the area on the work piece must be roughed up to allow the tip of the flaker to grip the flint and then push off small flakes from its inside edge. If you try to take off too large a flake you will find that you are not strong enough, so small flakes are better. If you are working on a flake work piece, each time you remove a small flake you can turn the work piece over and you will see a scar from the removal. This scar is an ideal platform to take a new flake from this side.

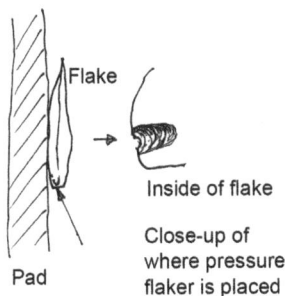

Fig. 83.

You can now make quite a few tools from your original flakes.

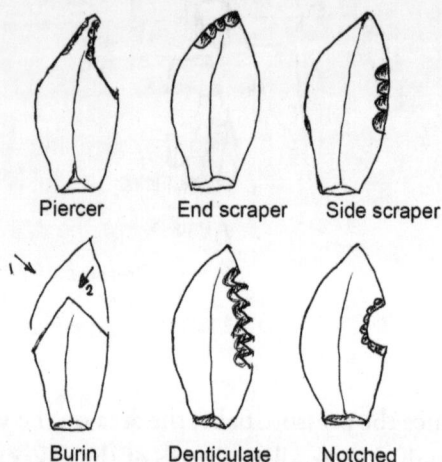

Fig. 84.

As you gain experience you can start trying to replicate the prehistoric tools you may have found.

These are the absolute basics for understanding how flint tools were made but the techniques should also enable you to at least make something at your first try. To progress to making a hand axe or an arrowhead requires more learning and considerable practice.

When I first started with John Lord and his son Will, who has made a number of very instructive videos, I was immediately taken back in time to see how our early ancestors lived and hunted. Later in my career, I was able to handle bifaces made nearly half a million years ago and this has given me the most wonderful interest that has remained ever since.

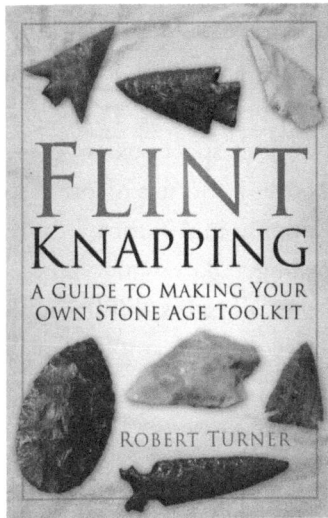

978-0-7524-8874-5

If you are really keen and would like further reading, I can recommend my book *Flint Knapping: A Guide to Making Your Own Stone Age Toolkit* (The History Press, 2013), which takes you through every stage required to produce professional flint tools. My book lists what rocks to use, how the conchoidal fracture works and how to get started. It takes you through the tools you need to make a start and which tools are needed to refine your knapping skills as you progress.

It shows you the basics of core production and flake and blade tools and then leads you into core tools like the axe and the adze. Modern tools are, however, used for fine work and you are shown the intricacies of pressure flaking and indirect percussion. Thinning of bifaces and arrowhead production requires a greater depth of skill, but, by following the notes, every aspect of knapping is ultimately possible. It just requires practice.

Many archaeological aspects are covered, especially flint mines and the recovery and use of other knapping stone, as well as flint knapping in America, heat treating of stone and, finally, recording and drawing your successes.

It also includes a full index, bibliography and glossary of terms, and has received many positive comments and customer reviews.

GLOSSARY

Barb	Side arms on the rear of an arrowhead
Blade	An elongated flake where the length is more than twice the width
Bladelet	A blade less than 12mm wide
BP (before present)	Before 1 January 1950
Bulb of percussion	A raised area that is the first part of the shock wave
Burin	A tool made on the end of blade
Clovis (blade)	Early American projectile point
Conchoidal fracture	A shell-shaped initial bump in the shock-wave fracture of a flint
Core	The piece of flint that has had flakes or blades removed from it
Cortex	A rough white or brownish external layer on flint

Crypto-crystalline	Material having no internal structure
Debitage	Waste material or flakes from the knapping process
Denticulate	V-shaped retouch on a flake or blade to make a saw-blade profile
Discoidal	Circular
Distal end	The end of a flake or blade furthest from the point of percussion
Dorsal side	The outside of a flake being removed from a core
Flake	The small piece of flint removed from a flint nodule by percussion
Fulsome (blade)	Early American projectile point
Knapping	The art of creating tools by the percussion of flint
Levallois	Neanderthal method of making a cutting tool or arrowhead
Lithic	Latin for flint
Microlith	Small worked flakes manufactured for composite tools
Nodule	Misshapen lump of flint
Ovate	Oval-shaped tool
Plano convex	One side flat and the other side convex
Platform	The point where a percussion impacted
Proximal end	The end of a flake or blade nearest the point of percussion
Retouch	Secondary working on a blade or flake

Ripple	Secondary and further ripples following the bulb of percussion
Rough-out	The first stage of producing a flint axe
Solutrean	European time period
Tang	The tail end of an arrow to allow binding to a shaft
Tranchet	French for cut or a flake removed at 90 degrees on a tool
Truncated	Break the end of a blade or flake at 90 degrees
Ventral side	The inside of a blade or flake when removed from a core

BIBLIOGRAPHY

Andrefsky Jr, W., *Lithics: Macroscopic Approaches to Analysis*,
   Cambridge University Press, 1998.

Barton, K., *Blackpatch Flint Mine Excavation*, Sussex
   Archaeological Collections, 1922.

Bordaz, J., *Tools of the Old and New Stone Age*, David & Charles
   Ltd, 1970.

British Museum, *Flint Implements: An Account of Stone Age
   Techniques and Cultures*, British Museum Press, 1968.

Butler, C., *Prehistoric Flintwork*, The History Press, 2005.

Edmonds, M., *Stone Tools and Society: Working Stone in Neolithic
   and Bronze Age Britain*, Routledge, 1995.

Forrest, A., *Masters of Flint*, Terence Dalton Limited, 1983.

Frieman, C., & B. Eriksen, *Flint Daggers in Prehistoric Europe*,
   Oxbow Books, 2015.

Justice, N., & S. Kudlaty, *Field Guide to Projectile Points of the
   Midwest*, Indiana University Press, 2001.

Knowles, F., 'Stone-Worker's Progress: A Study of Stone Implements in the Pitt Rivers Museum', *Occasional Papers on Technology*, 6, University of Oxford, 1953.

Kooyman, B., *Understanding Stone Tools and Archaeological Sites*, University of Calgery Press, 2001.

Lord, J., *The Nature and Subsequent Uses of Flint: The Basis of Lithic Technology*, self-published, 1993.

McCarthy, F., *Australian Aboriginal Stone Implements*, Australian Museum Trust, 1976.

Oakley, K., *Man the Toolmaker*, Natural History Museum Publications, 1972.

Pitts, M., *Later Stone Implements*, Shire Publications, 1980.

Roe, D., *Prehistory*, Macmillan, 1970.

Scott-Jackson, J., *Lower and Middle Palaeolithic Artefacts from Deposits Mapped as Clay-with-flints: A New Synthesis with Significant Implications for the Earliest Occupation of Britain*, Oxbow Books, 2000.

Shepherd, W., *Flint: Its Origin, Properties and Uses*, Faber & Faber, 1972.

Shreeve, J., *The Neanderthal Enigma: Solving the Mystery of Modern Human Origins*, William Morrow, 2000.

Stanford, D., & B. Bradley, *Across Atlantic Ice: The Origin of America's Clovis Culture*, University of California Press, 2012.

Turner, R., *Flint Knapping: A Guide to Making Your Own Stone Age Toolkit*, The History Press, 2013.

Waddington, C., *The Joy of Flint: An Introduction to Stone Tools and Guide to the Museum of Antiquities Collection*, University of Newcastle, 2004.

Waldorf, D., *The Art of Flint Knapping*, 4th Edition, self-published, 2006.

Waldorf, D., *Guide to Flint Axes*, self-published, 2007).

Waldorf, D., *Guide to Flint Daggers*, self-published, 2007).

ABOUT THE AUTHOR

Robert Turner and his wife Gillian live in West Sussex and are both members of Worthing Archaeological Society and Sussex Archaeological Society. Robert is also a flint knapper and a member of the Lithics Society, and sometimes works with professional archaeologists. He runs flint courses at Butser Iron Age Village, was a tutor for Sussex University, and has over the years lectured and demonstrated flint tools to local societies, schools and history groups. He also teaches at schools.